THE PROSE SERMONS OF THE BOOK OF JEREMIAH

A Redescription of the Correspondences with Deuteronomistic Literature
in the Light of Recent Text-critical Research

SOCIETY
OF BIBLICAL
LITERATURE

DISSERTATION SERIES

J. J. M. Roberts, Old Testament Editor
Charles Talbert, New Testament Editor

Number 83

THE PROSE SERMONS OF THE BOOK OF JEREMIAH
A Redescription of the Correspondences with Deuteronomistic Literature
in the Light of Recent Text-critical Research

by
Louis Stulman

Louis Stulman

THE PROSE SERMONS OF THE BOOK OF JEREMIAH

A Redescription of the Correspondences
with Deuteronomistic Literature in the Light of
Recent Text-critical Research

Scholars Press
Atlanta, Georgia

THE PROSE SERMONS OF THE BOOK OF JEREMIAH

A Redescription of the Correspondences with Deuteronomistic Literature
in the Light of Recent Text-critical Research

Louis Stulman

BS
1525.2
.S78
1986

Ph.D., 1982
Drew University

Advisor:
Paul A. Riemann

Library of Congress Cataloging-in-Publication Data

Stulman, Louis, 1953–
  The prose sermons of the Book of Jeremiah.

  (Dissertation series / Society of Biblical
Literature ; no. 83)
  Thesis (Ph.D.)—Drew University, 1982.
  Bibliography: p.
  Includes index.
  1. Bible. O.T. Jeremiah—Criticism and inter-
pretation, etc. 2. Bible. O.T. Deuteronomy—Criticism,
interpretation, etc. I. Title. II. Series: Dissertation
series (Society of Biblical Literature) ; no. 83.
BS1525.2.S78   1987   224'.206   86-1935
ISBN 0-89130-960-8
ISBN 0-89130-961-6 (pbk.)

Printed in the United States of America

Contents

Acknowledgments

This book stems directly from research done at Drew University for partial fulfillment of the Ph.D. degree. I would like to express my appreciation and thanks to Professor Paul A. Riemann, adviser of my dissertation committee, for his guidance, insights, and encouragement in so many ways. I am indebted to him and his wife, Joy Riemann, for their gracious hospitality and kindness, especially during the summer months of 1981.

Very grateful thanks are due to my mentor and friend Professor Herbert B. Huffmon for his constructive criticism and careful scholarly approach not only while this work was being prepared but also during my years of course work at Drew. His constant encouragement and friendship will always be appreciated.

I also want to acknowledge my appreciation to Professor Emanuel Tov who took time while in the States to be a member of my dissertation committee. I am grateful to him for his interest, criticism, and generosity on every occasion. His writings in many ways have served as a catalysis for the present work.

Finally, I owe thanks to Professor Robert R. Wilson who served as editor of this volume.

I dedicate this book to my wife, Kate, and to our three children, Nate, Tim, and Amy.

1

Introduction

New questions often arise where lines of inquiry intersect. The purpose of the present study is to investigate an intriguing instance of this in the prose sermons of the Book of Jeremiah. Since this is a relatively recent development, it will be well to begin with a brief account of the situation and the problem it has posed.

THE PROBLEM TO BE INVESTIGATED

The prose sermons are passages of highly rhetorical prose, varying a great deal in length and scattered at irregular intervals through the book. In the first half (chaps. 1-25) they tend to be interspersed with poetic oracles, and in the next section (Hebrew chaps. 26-45) with biographical narratives. None appear in the last sections of the book (Hebrew chaps. 46-52), which contain oracles against foreign nations and appended materials.

These passages drew the attention of scholars early in the present century, when research into the composition of the book was first set on its present course. They seemed to share a diction, style and theological perspective which distinguished them from other parts of the book and associated them in some way with other parts of the biblical literature which are now commonly termed "Deuteronomistic."

The elaboration of these points of correspondence with Deuteronomistic literature has been one of the constant elements in the study of the prose sermons throughout the modern period. In fact this was one of the primary considerations which first led scholars to regard the prose sermons as a distinct stratum or corpus within the book, and it has continued to be a key factor in deciding which particular passages to assign to it. It appeared, moreover, to provide an essential clue to the date and provenience of these materials, and this in turn had obvious implications for the composition, history and provenience of the book as a whole. As a result, each succeeding generation of scholars has added new dimensions and expanded the list of observed correspondences, reflecting the changing and developing insights of biblical scholarship.

This detailed enumeration of correspondences with Deuteronomistic literature is the first of the intersecting lines of inquiry we have in mind. The second derives from relatively recent text-critical research. Here a new understanding of the nature of the Hebrew text underlying the Old Greek version (OG) of Jeremiah has led to a new perception of stages in the book's literary history.

Recent studies, prompted in part by the discovery of fragments of ancient manuscripts in the vicinity of the Dead Sea, have shown that the essential differences between the OG and the Masoretic text (MT) of Jeremiah derive from the Hebrew text the former translated, and not from changes introduced in the process of translation itself as scholars had generally assumed. This finding has had two significant and related consequences. It has spurred text critics to proceed by retroversion to recover as accurately as possible the Hebrew *Vorlage* which underlies the OG, since this is as important a witness to the text of the book as the MT. And it has led them to make a careful comparison of this retroverted OG *Vorlage* and the MT, since this makes it possible to identify stages in the textual transmission of the book which are in fact stages in its literary history.

Such comparisons have established that both of these text traditions derive ultimately from a common line, which subsequently diverged into two collateral branches. That some considerable time elapsed before this branching took place is indicated by the number of scribal errors they have in common; according to one estimate, the common line of transmission must have continued to the mid-fifth, or perhaps even the early fourth, century.

Subsequent to this branching, one of the collateral lines—the one represented by the MT—underwent a much more extensive process of expansion than the other. It is now evident that this is the reason the MT is significantly longer than the OG. In short, the MT now proves to represent a relatively late form of the text which derives from the Second Temple period.

It is obvious that the intersection of these quite different lines of inquiry would raise new issues. To this point scholars who have undertaken to describe the correspondences between the prose sermons and Deuteronomistic literature have done so largely on the basis of the MT. Now that it is realized that the MT is relatively late and expansionist, it is necessary to redescribe these correspondences to take this into account. This is all the more important because of the marked tendency in recent research to interpret the correspondences against the background of the exile (sixth century) or the late pre-exilic period. Since scholars have been proceeding largely on the basis of the MT, it necessarily follows that they have been depending in part upon data which cannot derive from so early a time.

THE FOCUS OF THE PRESENT STUDY

It is already apparent that the full implications of this new understanding of the text will be complex and wide-ranging, and well beyond the limits of a single study. But it seemed to us that we could make a reasonable start if we were simply to gather the many detailed observations which scholars have already made as they have compared the prose sermons and the Deuteronomistic literature, and make it our task to redescribe these in the light of the new text-critical findings. This has enabled us to make discrete observations about each of the literary stages, and to compare in detail their points of correspondence with Deuteronomistic literature. It has also enabled us to study the late expansions by themselves, and to compare the correspondences which they have introduced with those already to be found in the text they were elaborating.

What this entails is really a return to a prior question, namely the description of the essential data. At the present time discussions in the scholarly literature are understandably focused upon issues of interpretation. A few believe the data to indicate little more than a common prose style of the Jeremianic period. The majority think that data sufficient to establish some sort of association between the prose sermons and Deuteronomistic tradition. Some have argued that this association had already shaped the prophet himself, while others have concluded that the association developed later as the prophet's sayings were recast by his followers for a new situation in the exilic period. It goes without saying that the present study will not resolve all the issues currently in dispute. It will touch them all at a critical point, however, in view of the questions it poses. How close were the correspondences between the prose sermons and Deuteronomistic literature prior to the diverging of these lines of text transmission? It is evident that further debate about the nature and import of this association in the sixth century and earlier will be fruitless until this situation is clarified. A second question is hardly less important. How close were the correspondences between the later expansions to the text and Deuteronomistic literature? It will not be possible to judge how much importance to attach to the special circumstances of the late pre-exilic and exilic periods until we are able to give an answer to this question as well.

THE PLAN OF THE PRESENT STUDY

Before we could proceed to the redescription of the correspondences between the prose sermons and the Deuteronomistic literature, it was necessary to undertake several preliminary tasks. The first was to gather from the scholarly literature the observations which have already been made, and to organize them in a form that would be appropriate and useful. The results of our efforts are reported in Chap. 2. We decided to begin with a brief history of research because we found the historical context and the basic thrust of each scholar's approach to be important factors in understanding how these observations had been developed. Our account covers the period from the 1901 commentary of Bernhard Duhm, a work which in many repects provided the major impetus for the line of inquiry we are tracing, to the recent two-volume study by Winfried Thiel (1973, 1981). We have summarized these observations at the end of Chapter 2 by offering a catalog of words and phrases and a resumé of other kinds of correspondences.

While drawing up the catalog of words and phrases, we realized we would have to decide what to include and how best to organize it. At one point we considered limiting the list to diction attested more than once in the Deuteronomistic historical work (Dtr) as defined in the study of Martin Noth. We eventually decided to include virtually all the correspondences in diction which scholars have employed, and to group these according to four "types": (1) diction attested more than once in Dtr, (2) diction attested only once in Dtr, (3) diction unattested in Dtr but attested in Deut 4:44-29:1, and (4) diction not attested in either but said to resemble Deuteronomistic diction. In the end the distinction between (1) and (2) turned out to be the least helpful. But (3) enabled us to make some interesting observations, and (4) was particularly important. In fact it led to one of the most significant findings of the study.

The other preliminary task was more complex, because it involved the analysis of the text of each passage. It was necessary to decide first which passages to include, since scholars are not entirely agreed. On this matter we allowed ourselves to be guided by the general consensus, since what we required was a selection sufficiently representative to allow a reasonably coherent analysis. We are satisfied that the nineteen passages we have chosen provide this, even though they omit a few which some scholars have included, and include a few which some scholars have assigned elsewhere.

The next step was to take the OG text of each passage and proceed by a process of retroversion to the Hebrew *Vorlage* which underlies it. The rationale for this, and the principles and procedure we followed, are discussed in more detail in the introduction to Chapter 3. Both the rationale and the procedure are now well established for the Book of Jeremiah, but there have been no published retroversions of the OG texts of the prose sermons along these lines, so far as we are aware, apart from the study of Jer 27 by Emanuel Tov.

We have represented the results of our work in Chapter 3 by providing an edited text of each passage which distinguishes the readings which the OG *Vorlage* shares with the MT from readings which are represented by the MT alone.[1] This makes it possible to distinguish the literary stages of the text, prior to and subsequent to the divergence of the lines of text transmission. In order to avoid long and cumbersome phrases each time these literary stages are mentioned, we have adopted sigla to represent them. The MT of the prose sermons is designated C, following common usage.[2] Readings peculiar to the MT are designated C+. Readings common to the MT and the OG *Vorlage* are designated C'. In terms of their literary history, the order is of course the reverse. C' represents the earlier stage, prior to the branching of the lines of text transmission. C+ represents additions made subsequently to one of the branching lines. This produced the later literary stage, which is represented by C (= MT).

Once we had completed this preliminary work, we were ready to proceed to the task of redescription, examining each of the passages in turn. We have reported our findings in Chapter 3 by marking all the pertinent matters of diction in our edited text, where the readings of C' and C+ are readily distinguished, and summarizing the data in tabular form. Other kinds of correspondence are discussed in the commentary which follows each passage, and related to the appropriate literary stage.

It soon became clear to us that the analysis of diction in particular should be carried a step further. We assembled the data we had gathered

---

[1]Other differences are marked by an asterisk or discussed in notes.

[2]This siglum derives from Mowinckel, who employed it to refer to the third of the literary sources he had identified in the book; see further p. 10. Following Mowinckel the prose sermons have often been referred to as the "C stratum" or the "C source."

from each passage and reorganized it to achieve an overview of the literary stages of the corpus as a whole. This made it possible to determine how evenly Deuteronomistic diction is distributed throughout the corpus in the readings of C', C+ and C, and to make a detailed comparison of each of these in terms of the frequency, density, variety and type of Deuteronomistic diction they employ. The details of our analysis are reported in Chapter 4. Without anticipating our conclusions, we can say that distinguishing characteristics were observed in each stage, and that the differences between the earlier stage (C') and the later expansions (C+) were especially striking. This led us to explore some of the other characteristics of the later expansions, and we have discussed these in an excursus.

The concluding chapter offers a summary of our findings and the inferences we have ventured to draw.

2

The Correspondences between the Prose Sermons and Deuteronomistic Literature as Enumerated in Modern Research

A BRIEF HISTORY OF RESEARCH

The study of the prose sermons in Jeremiah cannot easily be separated from the study of the book as a whole. It was in fact the larger question of the composition of the book and its literary history which first led scholars to regard the prose sermons as a distinct corpus or stratum within the whole. This has continued to be an important factor in the discussion ever since.

The modern discussion of the literary and historical problems involved in the composition of the Book of Jeremiah takes as its point of departure the works of Bernhard Duhm and Sigmund Mowinckel. Duhm offered the first detailed analysis of the literary strata in his 1901 commentary *Das Buch Jeremia*.[1] He identified three types of material in the book. Two were primary literary strata; the third was really a residual category, including everything which had not been assigned to the other two. When Duhm undertook to characterize this rather diffuse third category, he observed that much of the material was sermonic in style, rhetorical and stereotyped in diction, and closely related to the editorial sections of the Former Prophets. It was observations of this sort which eventually led Mowinckel to refine the analysis and identify yet a third literary stratum in the book.[2]

The primary literary strata Duhm identified were (1) poetic sayings of Jeremiah and (2) a biography of the prophet in prose. The first comprised

---

[1] Bernhard Duhm, *Das Buch Jeremia* (Tübingen and Leipzig: J. C. B. Mohr, 1901).

[2] Sigmund Mowinckel, *Zur Komposition des Buches Jeremia* (Kristiania: Jacob Dywad, 1914).

about sixty poems, only a portion of the poetic materials in the book. These were regarded as the only authentic oracles in the book, with the exception of the prose letter to the exiles in Babylon (chap. 29).[3] The main index of these oracles was their conventional form, that of a dirge in 3:2 meter (*qînah* meter). He believed he had found in the sharpness and originality of these poems an unequivocal criterion by which to differentiate this group from the remaining unauthentic sayings. The second— Baruch's life of Jeremiah—was thought to comprise only about 220 verses of the present book, and to provide some reliable information about the life of Jeremiah, the conflicts he encountered, and the suffering he endured. Originally an independent work, it was only several hundred years later joined to the oracles of Jeremiah (now found in chaps. 1-25), and it now forms the basis of chaps. 26-45.[4]

This analysis left a residual category of miscellaneous later additions bulking larger than the first two combined. Duhm sought to identify the literary style, central ideas, theology, and recensional history of this non-Jeremianic material. Both in language and in point of view, he saw a striking affinity between the editorial segments of Jeremiah and the Deuteronomistic parts of the Former Prophets.[5] The supplements occupy themselves mainly with what is reported in 2 Kings concerning Northern Israel and Judah; they speak the same language and represent the same views. Thus one must conclude, argued Duhm, that the same hand is to be found in both literary corpora.[6]

The supplementary materials are characteristically written in a sermonic style. This is evident from the predominantly rhetorical vocabulary and stereotyped phraseology. In this respect Duhm asserted that these passages are actually sermonic expositions placed in the mouth of the prophet, or strictly speaking in the mouth of Yahweh, with introductory and concluding prophetic formulae (etc. כה אמר יהוה, נאם יהוה).[7] Their literary worth is slight, in that they lack originality and depend heavily upon older sources (such as Deuteronomy, Ezekiel, 2 Isaiah, 3 Isaiah). The original purpose of this kind of literary engagement was to create an instructive and edifying book (*Lehr- und Erbauungsbuch*) which would help the populace better to understand their religious and historical roots.[8]

---

[3]Duhm, p. xii.
[4]Ibid., pp. xiv-xvi.
[5]Ibid., p. xx.
[6]Ibid., p. x.
[7]Ibid., pp. xvif.
[8]Ibid., p. xvi.

The prominent theme of the editors' work is the incessant sins of the people, thought of primarily in terms of idolatry, and the inevitable result of such wrongdoing, namely, the catastrophe of Judah and the exile of 587. This motif was designed to help the readers understand why the exile had occurred and why the present people of God were in a distressful situation which seemed to contradict their relationship with God. In addition, it was employed to put the readers on guard against, and in fear of, similar offenses in their own time. Therefore, they were admonished not to transgress God's laws (the Sabbath regulations, the laws concerning manummission of Hebrew slaves, etc.).[9] Concerns of this sort, contended Duhm, belong to the post-exilic period, as does the prominent legalistic piety, with its dogma of retribution. "Their theology is that of legalism, the Torah is their be-all and end-all."[10] Accordingly, he reasoned that all of the editors' supplements, with perhaps the exception of chapter 52, derive from the post-exilic period and were continually added to the words of the prophet and the biography of Baruch through the long history of transmission until about the second century B.C.E.[11]

Duhm's treatment of Jer 11 is representative of his understanding of the editorial activity in the book as a whole.[12] The chapter exhibits the sermonic style which is characteristic of the residual material throughout the book, and its theological perspective conforms to that of the post-exilic period. Here God commissions Jeremiah to summon the people to obey the Deuteronomistic law. At the conclusion of the sermon God informs the prophet of his decree to bring total destruction upon the people of Judah for their disobedience to the ancestral covenant. Verses 3-5 contain words, themes and formulae reminiscent of Deut. The curse formula in vs. 3 corresponds to Deut 27:26; vs. 4 derives from Deut 4:20; and vs. 5 complies with the law given to all Israel in Deut 27:26. In the verses that follow, Jeremiah is told to wander through the cities of Judah and to act as God's emissary for the Deuteronomic law. Moreover, the words of the covenant which Yahweh had brought upon the disobedient fathers (vs. 8) are the threats that the Deuteronomist pronounced on those who do not observe the Law (27:28-30). In vs. 10 there emerges the Deuteronomistic view that under Josiah the people accepted Deuteronomy and its dictates, while under Jehoiakim the people of God reverted to the

---

[9]Ibid.
[10]Ibid., p. xviii.
[11]Ibid., p. x.
[12]Ibid., pp. 106ff.

sins of the earlier time. Jeremiah, Duhm asserted, knows nothing of this kind of sinfulness of Jehoiakim. The chapter as a whole assumes that the prophet has been entrusted by Yahweh with the promulgation and advocacy of the Law and has had an important part in the Deuteronomic reform. This representation of Jeremiah by the editor is entirely fictitious. Consequently, Duhm judged 11:1-14 to be an ad hoc composition; only in vv 15f. is a genuine Jeremianic kernel preserved.

The analysis which Sigmund Mowinckel proposed in his 1914 monograph *Zur Komposition des Buches Jeremia* took its start from Duhm's work. Mowinckel identified three major sources in the book which he designated as source A, an authentic Jeremianic tradition found mostly in poetry, source B, a block of biographical prose, and source C, a block of generally unauthentic prose sermons which are the product of Deuteronomistic redaction. His sources A and B were clearly modeled upon Duhm's two primary literary strata. In fact his source B was virtually identical to Duhm's "Book of Baruch," even though Mowinckel attributed it—at least at first—to an anonymous admirer of the prophet.[13] His source A was considerably larger than Duhm's "poetic sayings of Jeremiah," since it was not restricted to poetry in *qînah* meter but included a larger body of prophetic poetry and occasionally even prose material (e.g., 1:11f., 13-16; 14:11-16; 16:1-13; 17:1-4; and 24:1-10 although listed with a question mark).[14] Mowinckel subjected the remainder of the book—Duhm's third residual category, less the material which had now been reassigned to source A (and a few passages to B)—to further analysis. Here he identified a "Deuteronomistic C source" which is the focus of our attention in this study, a corpus of salvific sayings in chaps. 30-31 (designated source D), various interpolations and glosses, and several other large blocks of material such as the oracles against the foreign nations (chaps. 46-51).

What Mowinckel had done in marking out a "source C" was to identify the prose sermons for the first time as a distinct literary stratum, and to describe their typical introductory rubrics, style, diction, vocabulary, and even their use of conventional structure. He assigned to this source 7:1-

---

[13]Subsequently in *Prophecy and Tradition* (Oslo: Jacob Dywad, 1946), Mowinckel ascribed source B to Baruch rather than to an anonymous admirer of the prophet (p. 21).

[14]That Mowinckel's source A included several prose passages and thus was not an exclusively poetic block of material is often overlooked by scholars. See, for example, William L. Holladay, "Prototype and Copies: A New Approach to the Poetry-Prose Problem in the Book of Jeremiah," *Journal of Biblical Literature* 59 (1960):353.

8:3; 11:1-5, 9-14; 18:1-12; 21:1-10; 25:1-11a; 32:1f., 6-16, 24-44: 34:1-7, 8-22; 35:1-19 and 44:1-14; all of these passages have an introductory formula such as הדבר אשר היה אל ירמיהו מאת יהוה ("The word which came [lit. was] to Jeremiah from Yahweh"). Jer 27:1-22; 29:1-23; 3:6-13; 22:1-5; 39:15-18 and 45:1-5 were also assigned to source C although they lack the characteristic introductory sentence; he observed that nearly all the passages in this second group have themes which derive from source B and occasionally from source A.

With few exceptions (21:1-10 and 34:1-8) the C materials are not oracles (or prophetic sayings) but speeches. As speeches they are written in rhetorical prose, which he found to be generally very dull and lacking in enthusiasm.[15] These prose addresses employ a relatively limited vocabulary and are characterized particularly by their monotonous and impoverished style; they show little interest in describing the occasion or situation. Furthermore, they exhibit a conventional structure which in individual speeches varies only in matters of detail. Mowinckel characterized this structure as having the following elements:

     i. Summons to repentance and conversion
    ii. Identification of wrongdoing
   iii. The result of the insolence: An inevitable judgment.[16]

These sermonic materials are remarkably similar to the Deuteronomistic parts of Deuteronomy, Judges, and the books of Samuel and Kings in both vocabulary and phraseology. For example:

"to provoke me to anger,"	למען הכעסני
"men of Judah and inhabitants of Jerusalem,"	איש יהודה וישבי ירושלם
"with a mighty hand and outstretched arm,"	יד חזקה וזרע נטויה
"to go after other gods,"	הלך אחרי אלהים אחרים
"in the cities of Judah and in the streets of Jerusalem,"	בערי יהודה ובחוצות ירושלם
"to burn incense to Baal,"	קטר לבעל.

---

[15]Mowinckel, *Komposition,* p. 33.
[16]Ibid., p. 34.

The C material showed itself to be Deuteronomistic not only by its language and rhetorical style but also by its major motifs and concept of religion. Mowinckel agreed with Duhm that the major theme is the uninterrupted sins of Judah. Invariably the people of Judah walk in the ways of their ancestors and thus do that which is evil in the sight of God. The wrongdoing of the people of God is described in terms of apostasy, and this apostasy is virtually equivalent to idolatry. Judah has served "other gods" and therefore has done that which contradicts the fundamental requirements of the Deuteronomic covenant. A breach of Yahweh's ethical dictates is also accentuated to some degree in C, although not to the extent found in the undisputable oracles of Jeremiah. Moreover, the ethical interpretations of the divine commandments in C are much less poignant and pervasive than is typical of the A materials (e.g., 5:1f., 8-28, 30f.; 6:13-20 and passim). Although religion is understood in terms of "the observance of a divine law"[17] in source A, it never perceives the law as a "fixed, written and casuistically determined entity."[18] In contrast, source C has a more distinctly legalistic, indeed Deuteronomistic understanding of the deity's will. Therefore, Mowinckel concluded, C is close to the Deuteronomistic editorial sections of the Former Prophets in language, style, and in conception of religion.

Mowinckel found the understanding of the role and function of the prophet in source C also to be thoroughly Deuteronomistic and to differ essentially from the conception of the prophet which is evoked in source A. In the authentic oracles of Jeremiah, the prophet is depicted as a nonprofessional who feels himself under constraint to prophesy. His proclamation is essentially ethical in character and is thus addressed directly to the conduct of men. In addition, the *nabî* would warn the people of impending danger in order to give them the possibility of escaping the potential perial. The prophet was thus a watchman of the people (6:17). The conception of the prophet in the C material is entirely different. In the passages ascribed to this stratum, the prophet is seen as a member of a supernatural institution of bearers of piety and revelation in Israel, which extended through the classical epoch of the religion.[19] Beginning with Moses, the prophet *par excellence*, there existed in Israel an "uninterrupted institutional succession of inspired law-givers, proclaimers of

[17]Ibid., p. 36.

[18]Ibid.

[19]Ibid., p. 38.

God, ministers and preachers."[20] In this line of tradition, the message of
the prophet is one of reproof and admonition because of the people's
incessant violations of Yahweh's Law. Accordingly, the primary concern
of the Jeremiah of source C is to warn the people against the infringe-
ment of the Law, against idolatry and other offenses. His main admonish-
ment is thus: Do not violate Yahweh's Law, namely Deuteronomy, but
mend your ways and live in accordance with its demands.[21]

In general, C has rejected the complex and varied actions of the living
prophet in favor of a function as a moralistic and dogmatic preacher. It
sees him in the light of the unhistorical Deuteronomic conception of Law
and reproduces its words. C's monotony, said Mowinckel, has replaced A's
variety and diversity. C's impoverished language and content have sup-
planted the genuine Jeremiah's richness of ideas, thoughts, forms and
moods. The multifaceted personality of Jeremiah with its many expressions and perceptions has been transformed into a "shadowy figure"
("*Schattfigur*") proclaiming a dogmatic theology. In C nothing remains of
the man Jeremiah who appears before us alive and active in sources A and
B.[22]

Mowinckel found the contrast decisive: the C corpus comes from a
writer who recast the materials according to a particular viewpoint and a
specific scheme, whereas A preserved the genuine prophetic tradition. As
to the redaction history of source C, Mowinckel proposed that this stratum had been incorporated into the existing work of AB; that is to say,
"$R^J = R^{ABC}$ had already met with book AB and incorporated into it the
collection C."[23] He set ca. 400 B.C.E. as the possible *terminus a quo* for
the C material because its legalistic piety is characteristic of late Judaism.[24]

---

[20]Ibid.

[21]Ibid.

[22]Ibid., p. 39.

[23]Ibid., p. 52.

[24]Ibid., p. 57. It is helpful to recall that at the turn of the century,
when Duhm and Mowinckel raised the issue, there was a strong tendency
in scholarship to turn first to source criticism for a solution to problems
concerning the prehistory of the prophetic and historical books, and there
was general agreement that the literary redaction of biblical materials
had continued well into the Hellenistic period. These two features of early
twentieth research were in fact interrelated. The source-critical analysis
presented by Mowinckel, for example, found a great many hands involved
in the formation of the book of Jeremiah. For the compilation of chaps. 1-

In the same year that Mowinckel's monograph appeared, Gustav
Hölscher published his *Die Profeten*, which dealt briefly with the composition of the Book of Jeremiah.[25] The basic outlines of Duhm's analysis are
readily discerned in Hölscher's account, and in some respects he followed
Duhm more closely than Mowinckel. At the same time he departed from
Duhm at a number of points; some of his ideas anticipated later develop-
ments, but others never came to be widely accepted. The core of his
argument was that the present book derived from a single redactor who
had at his disposal two *Vorlagen*, "I" material ("*Ich-Berichte*") and "he"
material ("*Er-Berichte*"). The "I" material was comparable to but more
inclusive than Mowinckel's source A and Duhm's category of authentic
oracles; to some degree he anticipated here the later work of Rudolph.[26]
Hölscher assigned to this group the bulk of chaps. 1-19:13; 20:7-18; 21:11-
25:1f.; 27; 30-33; 35; for the most part, this *Vorlage* contained prophetic
poetry and discourses, as well as discrete accounts of the prophetic
actions. The "he" material was virtually identical to Duhm's "Book of
Baruch"; chaps. 19:14-20:6; 21:1-10; 26; 36-45; 51:59-64 were assigned to
this block of tradition. The redactor, Hölscher suggested, lived no later
than the Persian period; he combined and arranged his sources, yet not
without leaving his own stamp on the material, as is evidenced primarily
by the numerous stereotyped phrases. Moreover, he added to these two
Vorlagen his own compositions, which usually took the form of prose
sermons or discourses. Although Hölscher identified many of the stereotyped expressions employed in these sermons (and the two main sources)
as Deuteronomistic, his redactor was not a Deuteronomic or Deuteronomistic editor. Accordingly, he observed that "in style and in range of
ideas, these secondary prose speeches are closely in accord with Deuter-

---

45, he assumed the participation of at least eight redactors or editors
(R^A, R^B, R^C, R^D, R^{AB}, R^{ABC}, R^{ABCD}, R^J) in addition to numerous
interpolations and glosses. The complexities of the literary history of the
book suggested to him that the process of redaction must have continued
for some time; this undoubtedly contributed to his assignment of the C
source to the post-exilic period. See Thiel, *Die deuteronomistische Redaktion von Jeremiah 1-25*, for an excellent discussion of Mowinckel's source-
critical analysis, pp. 11f.

[25] Gustav Hölscher, *Die Profeten: Untersuchungen zur Religionsgeschichte Israels* (Leipzig: R. Voightlanders, 1914), pp. 379ff.

[26] Rudolph's view that the editor of C was the chief redactor of the
book is a further point of contact with Hölscher; see below p. 17.

onomy; but they especially display a clear influence from Ezekiel."[27] The Jeremiah portrayed in these passages is a disciple of Ezekiel and a man whose ideal is the observance of the law.[28]

It was primarily the analysis of Mowinckel which influenced the course of subsequent research. Various aspects of his hypothesis were accepted by Skinner,[29] Horst,[30] Robinson,[31] Meinhold,[32] Pfeiffer,[33] and Rudolph.[34] The most influential of these was certainly Wilhelm Rudolph, whose commentary *Jeremia* appeared in 1947. It was his restatement of the hypothesis which provided the basis for much of the research which followed. Rudolph took over the basic outlines of Mowinckel's literary analysis, but his assignment of passages to each stratum was often different. He identified three sources which were designated, following Mowinckel, A,B, C.[35] Against Mowinckel, he did not recognize an independent D source in chaps. 30-31; instead he followed Paul Volz who had argued for the substantial authenticity and unity of these chapters. The oracles found there, as well as those in chaps. 46-49, he included in his A source. Thus Rudolph's A material came to include prophetic sayings ("*Spruche*") in the widest sense of the word. For the most part, these sayings are given without formal introductions or circumstantial details; they do, however, employ the prophetic formula כה אמר יהוה ("thus says Yahweh") at the beginning and occasionally at the end of the oracle. Rudolph's B source was somewhat more inclusive than Mowinckel's; he ascribed to B several passages which Mowinckel had assigned to C (see

---

[27]Ibid., p. 385.

[28]Ibid., p. 386.

[29]J. Skinner, *Prophecy and Religion. Studies in the Life of Jeremiah* (Cambridge: University Press, 1922), pp. 102, 107.

[30]F. Horst, "Die Anfänge des Propheten Jeremia," *Zeitschrift für die alttestamentliche Wissenschaft* 41 (1923): 94-153.

[31]Th. H. Robinson, "Baruch's Roll," *Zeitschrift für die alttestamentliche Wissenschaft* 42 (1924): 209ff.

[32]J. Meinhold, *Einführung in das Alte Testament* (Giesen, 1926), p. 231.

[33]R. H. Pfeiffer, *Introduction to the Old Testament* (New York: Harper & Row, 1941), pp. 500ff.

[34]W. Rudolph, *Jeremia* (Tübingen: J. C. B. Mohr, 1947).

[35]It is interesting to note that a year before Rudolph's commentrary was published, Mowinckel had turned to a more traditio-historical understanding of the composition of the book of Jeremiah. He replaced the word "source" with the term "traditionary circle." By using this traditio-historical term he presumably meant the circles in which oral tradition was preserved; see *Prophecy and Tradition*, p. 105.

below); moreover, he characterized it as a passion narrative ("*Leidens-geschichte*") rather than a general biography of the prophet. Rudolph followed Mowinckel in describing the C source as prose sermons exhibiting the monotonous and stereotyped Deuteronomistic style and language, and dealing with essentially the same basic theme: "Judah and Jerusalem or a certain segment of the people (34:8ff.) or the king (22:1-5; cf. 21:1-10) have met with destruction, because they have not hearkened to the words of Yahweh."[36] In addition to the three major sources, Rudolph identified several unauthentic oracles which only later came to be incorporated into the existing book of ABC.

Rudolph made several significant contributions with respect to the C materials. In the first place, he narrowed the number of passages attributable to C by assigning some to A and others to B: 3:6-13 (A); 27:1-22 (A); 29:1-32 (B); 32:6ff. (A); 34:1-7 (B); 39:15-18 (B); 44:1ff. (B); 45:1-5 (B). Thus, included in C were only 7:1-8:3; 11:1-14; 16:1-13; 17:19-27; 21:1-10; 22:1-5; 25:1-14; 34:8-22; 35:1ff. This circumscription and reclassification was based on two main factors: (1) the autobiographical sections (*Selbstberichte*) of the book (3:6-13; 27:1-22; 32:6ff.) were reassigned to source A owing to their richness of ideas, originality, and form;[37] and (2) the narrative accounts relating certain incidents in the prophet's life, which had been ascribed to C by Mowinckel (29:1-32; 34:1-7; 39:15-18; 44:1ff; 45:1-5), were reckoned to lack the necessary indices or characteristics to justify their inclusion in the C stratum. Rudolph found all the prose sermons of this narrowly defined corpus to relate the common theme of Judah's disobedience to Yahweh's words (and the judgment which this disobedience entailed) in the same prolix and repetitious style and with similar Deuteronomistic phraseology. Moreover, unlike Mowinckel, he ascertained that genuine Jeremianic themes and sayings lie ultimately behind the C material, but at the same time agreed with Mowinckel that Deuteronomistic influence had introduced essential shifts in meaning which to varying degrees distorted Jeremiah's own intention.[38] For example, the theological ideas expressed in the speeches of 7:1-8:3 and 22:1-5 concerning the cultus, the deity, and morality are entirely consistent with those which emerge in the undisputable oracles of the prophet; notwithstanding, Judah's sins are described in the familiar Deuteronomistic language, with the people of God being blamed for violating definite Deuteronomic commandments.

---

[36] Rudolph, *Jeremia*, p. xv.

[37] That is, "addresses/lectures in the exilic synagogue" (p. xvi).

[38] Rudolph, *Jeremia*, p. xv.

Furthermore, Rudolph put back the time of composition of the C material to the exilic period. Against Mowinckel's post-exilic dating, he argued that the form, ideas and concerns of passages ascribed to the C stratum are representative of the exilic community: "We have here plainly before us a work of the exilic Deuteronomist."[39]

Lastly, he ascribed to the author of C the role of chief redactor of the book of Jeremiah in its present form, allowing, to be sure, for some later interpolations (e.g., 10:1-16; 50:1-51:58) and glosses, but no further systematic redaction.[40] He based this judgment on the observation that C's distinctive style, character, and introductory formula appear occasionally in A and B materials, and that chaps. 19 (B), 32 (A), and 44 (B) contain secondary material which bears the stamp of C.[41]

The study which J. Philip Hyatt published in 1951 basically took the issue which we have just mentioned as its starting point.[42] In essence the question was this: if the Deuteronomistic features of C were to be found elsewhere in the book, as Rudolph had indicated, how far did this influence reach and how extensively had it shaped the book? To answer this, Hyatt sought to isolate more precisely the nature and extent of this editorial factor, and in so doing found the activity of the Deuteronomistic editor to be much more pervasive and penetrating than had been previously recognized. Such an observation led him to reject the analysis of Mowinckel and Rudolph which had by and large restricted the Deuteronomistic activity to a relatively limited number of discrete passages and to argue instead that D "was responsible for making an edition of the book in one of its earlier stages."[43] It is significant that he no longer spoke of this

---

[39]Ibid., p. xvi. "Wir haben hier offenbar eine Arbeit der exilischen Deuteronomiker vor uns." It should be noted that in Rudolph's work an important shift occurred from viewing the growth and formation of the prose discourses as an essentially literary process, to assuming a more spontaneous development of these materials as the existing Jeremianic tradition was studied, taught and preached. Rudolph posited that these sermons took shape within the context of the exilic congregation, where they served to help the community to preserve and enhance its religious character. The C passages are thus "samples of addresses in the exilic synagogue" (p. xvi).

[40]Ibid., pp. xviiff.

[41]Ibid., p. xix.

[42]Hyatt, "The Deuteronomic Edition of Jeremiah," *Vanderbilt Studies in the Humanities* 1 (1951) : 71-95.

[43]Ibid., p. 76.

as the work of the "editor of C," as Rudolph had done, but employed instead a new siglum, D, to represent the Deuteronomistic editor of the book. It was still the case, of course, that many of his observations about D were drawn from the C corpus and so are immediately relevant to the present study.

In order to identify the Deuteronomistic elements in the edition, Hyatt, like his predecessors, employed criteria of diction, style and theology. He endeavored, however, to clarify and refine each criterion, particularly in its association with the first and later editions of Deuteronomy and the editorial parts of the Former Prophets.[44] His indices of Deuteronomistic diction were categorized and subdivided into three groups: phrases which appear in the Deuteronomistic sections of the historical books as well as in Deuteronomy; longer phrases which show a particularly close relationship to Deuteronomy (especially chap. 28); and stereotyped phrases which occur in Jeremiah frequently in combination with the above categories but rarely or not at all in Deuteronomy or the editorial parts of Joshua through 2 Kings. Regarding style, D shows a tendency to employ a limited number of stereotyped words and word-combinations in a repetitious and monotonous manner and in a generally parenetic tone. Its own ad hoc compositions most frequently appear as speeches and prayers. With respect to ideas, D shows a distinctive theology and *Anschauung*. First and foremost, D demands of the people of God unwavering and exclusive allegiance to God. Idolatry, the worship of foreign gods (אלהים אחרים), is thus one of the gravest acts of wrongdoing. Pure worship is fulfilled by eliminating any syncretistic element in the cultus and by offering sacrifice exclusively in the Jerusalem temple. Moreover, D has its own distinctive theology of history, expressed most clearly as divine retribution operative in the sphere of human behavior. According to Hyatt, "Yahweh always punishes the wicked and rewards the righteous."[45] The exile of the people of God and the desolation wrought in Judah are explained solely in terms of this doctrine of retribution. D's theology of history also includes the promise of restoration from exile and future prosperity (e.g., 32:16-44). In sum, D affirms that "all of history is under the control of Yahweh."[46]

Hyatt's approach to the history of the book raised several new issues, including the method and sources employed by D and his motive or

---

[44]Ibid., pp. 76ff.
[45]Ibid., p. 77.
[46]Ibid., p. 92.

Tendenz in editing the book. For Hyatt, the Deuteronomistic editor of Jeremiah made use of a variety of methods in preparing his work. This editorial process was analogous to that employed by the Deuteronomistic editor(s) of Deuteronomy-2 Kings. D sometimes preserved original Jeremianic oracles, prayers and symbolic actions without significant change (e.g., 3:1-5, 12b-14a, 19-25; 4:1ff; 5:1-17, 20-30 and passim), providing, for example, only the framework for the older material; at other times he revised or rewrote his sources, introducing significant shifts in meaning which distorted their original intention; moreover, he sometimes took the liberty to create his own ad hoc compositions (e.g. 17:19-27; 24:1-10). It was very common for the Deuteronomistic editor to incorporate "original materials unchanged within sections composed or revised by him . . . ; 1:15-19 (17 being genuine); 7:1-8:3 (7:29 being a direct quotation); 11:1-17 (15-16 being genuine); and 16:1-13, 16-18 (16-17 being authentic)."[47]

Although Hyatt found it impossible to recover the Deuteronomistic editor's sources with complete confidence, he suggested in general terms that D had at his disposal Baruch's scroll rewritten at the prophet's dictation, various collections of Jeremianic materials preserved by Baruch and/or others, and Baruch's passion narrative (*Leidensgeschichte*) of Jeremiah.[48]

The primary intention and *Tendenz* of the editor of Jeremiah, according to Hyatt, was to "show how Jeremiah, the outstanding prophet at the time of Judah's decline and downfall, was in general agreement with the ideas and purposes of the Deuteronomic school."[49] That is to say, Jeremiah is depicted as an ardent evangelist for the Josianic reform and its ideals, when in fact he probably never supported this religious renewal. The editor achieved this objective primarily by inserting speeches in the mouth of the prophet. In these addresses Jeremiah summons the covenant people to obey the Deuteronomistic commandments and makes their existence as a nation contingent upon their obedience to these regulations (e.g., 17:19-27). Furthermore, the Jeremiah of these discourses explains the exile and the devastation of Judah as the direct consequence of the people's transgression of Deuteronomistic ideals.

Following Rudolph (against Mowinckel), Hyatt proposed that the Deuteronomistic editor of Jeremiah was active during the time of the Babylonian exile, around the year 550 B.C.E. This date was based on a

---

[47]Ibid., p. 94.

[48]Ibid., pp. 92f.

[49]Ibid., pp. 91f.

number of considerations, including the vague and general tone of D's prophecies of return from exile, the lack of evidence in D's work that the exile had ended, and the striking similarities between D and the exilic Deuteronomistic editor of Deuteronomy and the historical books.[50]

Soon after Hyatt's article appeared, Enno Janssen published his *Juda in der Exilszeit.*[51] Janssen concluded that the prose sermons derive from the activity of Deuteronomistic preachers in the exilic period and advanced a form-critical case for this contention. In this he was following Rudolph, who had already intimated in 1947 that the growth and development of the prose sermons ought not to be viewed solely as a literary process. Janssen proposed a spontaneous oral development of the Jeremianic tradition as it was employed in the community of faith. Deuteronomistic preachers used the tradition for their own purposes as they taught in the synagogue, and in so doing they reinterpreted it according to the pressing needs and concerns of the community. The most compelling anxiety of the exilic people of God was to know why Judah had met with such utter destruction. Like the author of the great historical work, the repositories of prophetic tradition explained the ruin of Judah as God's just punishment for the people's apostasy and disobedience. Thus in each speech one can learn that the nation is disobedient to the Law and that therefore judgment is imminent. Consequently, the prose sermons grew out of a situation in which Deuteronomistic preachers engaged the tradition to help their community come to terms with the tragic historical realities of 587 and beyond.[52]

Although Janssen argued for a Deuteronomistic origin of the prose sermons on linguistic and theological grounds, as Mowinckel and Rudolph had done, he was the first to adduce form-critical evidence for the case.

---

[50]Ibid., p. 91.

[51]Enno Janssen, *Juda in der Exilszeit. Ein Beitrag zur Frage der Entstehung des Judentums* (Göttingen: Vandenhoeck and Ruprecht, 1956), pp. 20f., 105ff.

[52]Janssen argued that in the exilic period Judah, far from being barren and unproductive, was a locus of considerable theological and literary activity. It was in this milieu, he maintained, that the prose sermons in the book of Jeremiah received their present form. He adduced three primary arguments for a Judaean provenience: (1) there are no clear indications of an expectation of return from exile in the materials; (2) the divine judgment is thought of in terms of the destruction of Judah and Jerusalem rather than exile to a foreign land; and (3) indigenous (Canaanite) cultic practices are represented as posing a fundamental threat to the covenant people's well-being.

He contended that "the speeches derive from the Deuteronomistic school. Their dependence on Deuteronomy can be perceived from the vocabulary and ideological content. The same thing can be affirmed with even greater certainty from the form."[53] The form of the Jeremianic speeches comprises the following elements:[54]

Chapter	Introduction	The Word of Yahweh in the Imperative: the Commandments	Statement of the Disobedience: the Description	Judgment/ Threats
Jer. 7	1-2	3-7	8-12	13f., 16ff.
Jer. 11	1-2	3-6	7-10	11, 17
Jer. 16	1	2-9	10-12	13ff.
Jer. 17	19-20	21-22	23-26	27
Jer. 18	1-5	6-11	12	(13-17)
Jer. 21	1-4a		4b-7	8-10
Jer. 22	1-2	3	4-5	6-9 in parts
Jer. 25	1-3	4-6	7	8-14
Jer. 34	8-12	13-14a	14b-16	17-22
Jer. 35	1-13a	13b	14-16	17ff.

Internally the individual speeches show some variation. In some sermons this form is clearly evident, while in others it is less prominent. The basic form, however, is virtually identical to that which underlies several discourses in Dtr. Note the following:[55]

Chapter	Introduction	Recital of Yahweh's Acts	Commandments/ Description of Disobedience	Threats and Promises
Josh. 1	1-2	3-5	6-8a	8b-9
Josh. 23	1-2	3-5	6-11	12-16
Judg. 2	10z	1-b	11-13	14-15
Sam. 12	7	8-13		
1 Kgs. 8	14	15-26		27ff.
2 Kgs. 17	7a	7b	8-17 21-41	18-20

---

[53]Janssen, *Exilszeit*, p. 108.
[54]Ibid., pp. 105ff.
[55]Ibid., p. 107.

The formal similarities between the speeches in the book of Jeremiah and those in the Deuteronomistic historical work as well as the linguistic and theological parallels between the two bodies of material led Janssen to conclude that both derive from the same exilic school.[56]

In his 1965 monograph *Die prophetischen Heilserwartungen im Alten Testament*[57] Siegfried Herrmann devoted a chapter to the examination of those passages in Jeremiah which contain salvific expectations or promises, and concluded that these also show a striking linguistic and conceptual affinity with the Deuteronomistic historical work. This was an aspect of the problem which had been largely unexplored; as our summaries have shown, previous scholars had tended to connect only the "legalistic" and "moralistic" aspects of the Jeremianic prose materials with Deuteronomistic tradition. It was Herrmann's contention that the Jeremiah of these sermonic pieces does not proclaim the inescapable demands of Yahweh, but instead poses Deuteronomistic alternatives (e.g., 17:24-27). Moreover, the speeches of this Jeremiah, couched in a distinctively didactic and verbose style, are entirely general and Deuteronomistic in nature: to turn from one's evil ways, to hearken to the voice of Yahweh, to do good and to seek Yahweh with a whole heart; "otherwise he [Yahweh] would destroy the people."[58] Thus Deuteronomistic theology appears here in the guise of prophetic discourses.

The sermons' *Anschauung,* Herrmann argued, is derived from Israel's past traditions, and specifically from its Deuteronomic and Deuteronomistic heritage. These traditions are assumed to have provided the present people of God with both a religious and moral standard for the past and a prospect for possibilities which would be realized as a program for the future. In 31:31-34, for example, this salvific program is described briefly. Deuteronomic and Deuteronomistic traditions and symbols serve as the basis for its realization. The program is depicted as a relationship between Yahweh and his people which is inaugurated by covenant renewal.

---

[56]Janssen's work represents a significant shift in the evaluation of the Deuteronomistic element in the book of Jeremiah. The Deuteronomistic activity is now seen, not as a distortion of the Jeremianic materials as earlier scholars had tended to view it, but rather as an adaptation of these oracles to a real situation, an adaptation which had an integrity of its own.

[57]Siegfried Herrmann, *Die prophetischen Heilserwartungen im Alten Testament,* Beiträge zur Wissenschaft vom Alten und Neuen Testament 5 (Stuttgart: W. Kohlhammer Verlag, 1965).

[58]Herrmann, *Heilserwartungen,* p. 190.

This notion has its roots in Dtr where covenant ceremonies occasionally appear at crucial junctures of Israel's history. With the new covenant, however, the expected conditional element recedes and the salvation-expectant (*heilserwartliche*) dimension emerges. Yahweh now endows his people with the ability and desire to obey his law. Moreover, the exhortation to love Yahweh earnestly, the idea of the Torah being internalized in Israel's heart, and the importance of knowing Yahweh all take as their point of departure motifs and matters of concern in Deuteronomy and Dtr. Thus Jeremiah—the last great prophet in Jerusalem whose doom (*unheilsgeschichtliche*) prophecies had been fulfilled—was transformed into a spokesman for Deuteronomistic ideals and salvific expectations.

Herrmann's study was followed by E. W. Nicholson's *Preaching to the Exiles*.[59] Nicholson adopted Janssen's basic thesis—that the prose sermons derive from the activity of Deuteronomistic preachers in the exilic period—and developed this into a working hypothesis for the Jeremianic prose tradition as a whole.[60] He also followed Herrmann in associating hope as well as judgment with the Deuteronomistic tradition. In his view, virtually all the prose material in the book took shape and assumed its present form at the hands of a circle of traditionists who employed certain sayings from the existing stock of Jeremianic oracles in order to address themselves to a "listening audience, more specifically, to gatherings which probably constituted the beginnings of what eventually developed into the institution of the synagogue."[61] These traditionists transformed the deposit of Jeremianic material according to their own kerygmatic and didactic needs and then reapplied the words of Yahweh to the ever new concerns of the exilic community (*golah*) in Babylon.[62]

---

[59] E. W. Nicholson, *Preaching to the Exiles: A Study of the Prose Tradition in the Book of Jeremiah* (New York: Schocken, 1971).

[60] Against Janssen, Nicholson has argued for a Babylonian provenience of the prose materials, as opposed to a Judaean. In support of this view he had adduced several arguments. Most important of these is the contention that the prose tradition exhibits a basic attitude of disparagement and antagonism toward the community which remained in Judah. The narrative complexes in Jer 26-36 and 40:7-44:30, as well as the single unit Jer 24, all indicate that the residents of Judah during the exilic period stood under the judgment of Yahweh. Conversely, the exiles in Babylon are depicted as representing the true remnant of Israel to whom Yahweh's grace and promises for the future are directed (pp. 127ff.).

[61] Nicholson, *Preaching*, p. 137.

[62] See n. 60 above for a further discussion of Nicholson's arguments for a Babylonian provenience.

Nicholson adduced a number of arguments for a Deuteronomistic provenience of the prose tradition of Jeremiah. With other proponents of the redaction hypothesis, he ascertained striking similarities in vocabulary, phraseology, and style between the Jeremianic prose sermons and the Deuteronomistic literature. Moreover, he found an analogous method employed by both literary bodies with regard to their treatment of the traditional materials. The persons who handled the Jeremianic sayings as well as those who were responsible for the prophetic traditions in Dtr seem to have used the available materials in similar ways: at times they employed oracles with little or no alteration; not infrequently they juxtaposed a nucleus of the original material beside their own composition; these same "theologians" at times composed their own ad hoc creations, or constructed their works perhaps on the basis of the memory of an original oracle.[63] Nicholson also detected in the literary structure of the Jeremianic prose discourses and the sermons in Deuteronomy and Dtr important similarities which he traced to their common utilization of the covenant form as root metaphor. With the exception of the historical retrospect, which occupies a more prominent place in Deuteronomy and Dtr, the same underlying covenant structure is clearly attested in many of the speeches in Deuteronomy, the great Deuteronomistic historical work, and Jeremiah.[64]

Also important for Nicholson's contention are the virtually identical theological motifs which find expression in both the Jeremianic prose tradition and in the Deuteronomistic historical work. First, several prose discourses in Jeremiah are based on, or are direct reproductions of an important Deuteronomistic *Prophetenaussage* concerning Israel's (*un*)*heilsgeschichtliche* experience. This "prophetic declaration" can be summarized as follows: Yahweh warns his people by "his servants the prophets" to turn from their evil ways and keep his commandments; Israel, however, rejects the word of Yahweh spoken by the prophets; *ergo,* Yahweh judges his people (e.g., 2 Kgs 17:13-18; Jer 7:25-34; 25:4-11; 26:4-6; 29:17-19; 35:15, 17; 36:1-31; 44:4-6).[65] Second, the Jeremianic prose tradition reflects the Dtr kerygma, namely, if Israel would "turn again" (שוב) to Yahweh, then he would have compassion upon his people and restore their well-being, and ultimately cause them to realize once again their true existence as his chosen heritage (Deut 4:29-31; 30:1-6; 1 Kgs

---

[63]Nicholson, *Preaching,* pp. 30ff., 137f.

[64]Ibid., pp. 32ff.

[65]Ibid., pp. 55ff.

8:46-50; cf. 2 Kgs 25:27-30; Jer 18:1-12 and especially vv 7-10).[66] The prose sermons, however, develop the original Dtr kerygma further and assert that Israel's "turning again" is "now assured by Yahweh himself who now takes the initiative so Israel *will* 'turn again' (Jeremiah 24:7; cf. 29:12)."[67] Jer 31:31-34 and 32:36-41 reflect an even further (eschatological) development of this kerygma by affirming that Yahweh will give Israel "one heart and one way" to fear him, and will place his "fear" in the hearts of his people for the sole purpose that they not "turn away" (שוב) from him (32:38-40); Yahweh will thus endow the people of Israel with the "heart desire" and ability to live in accordance with his Torah. Lastly, the Deuteronomistic hopes for reactivation of the Davidic promises to which Jehoiachin's release gave rise[68] emerge in a number of passages in the Jeremianic tradition which "contain promises for the future centering on the kingship or specifically on the promises to David" (Jer 23:1-4; 3:15; 30:8f.; 33:14-16; 33:17-26).[69]

Winfried Thiel's two monographs—which represent the most extensive discussion of the Deuteronomistic redaction of Jeremiah 1-45 to appear in recent years—are essentially an elaboration of Hyatt's thesis.[70] At the same time, his assessment of the theological perspective of this redaction is more positive than Hyatt's had been, reflecting the judgment of more recent research; the redactor addressed the real needs of an actual situation. Thiel proposes that the difficulty in dealing with the various blocks of Jeremianic traditions could be alleviated if one would proceed from the premise that Jeremiah 1-45 has undergone a thorough Deuteronomistic redaction, or to put it another way, that a Deuteronomistic redactor is responsible for preparing an edition of Jeremiah in one of its earlier forms during the exilic period.

In order to identify the activity of the Deuteronomistic redactor, Thiel, like his predecessors, has employed criteria of diction, style, form, and theology. Regarding diction, his criterion is more rigorous than previous

---

[66]Ibid., pp. 75ff.

[67]Ibid., p. 81.

[68]G. von Rad, *Old Testament Theology*, vol. 1, trans. D. M. G. Stalker (New York: Harper & Row, 1962), pp. 242ff.

[69]Nicholson, *Preaching*, p. 87.

[70]W. Thiel, "Die deuteronomistische Redaktion des Buches Jeremia" (Th.D. dissertation, Humboldt-Universität, Berlin, 1970); *Die deuteronomistische Redaktion von Jeremia 1-25* (Wageningen: Neukirchener, 1973); *Die deuteronomistische Redaktion von Jeremia 26-45* (Düsseldorf: Neukirchener, 1981).

studies in that he distinguishes Deuteronomic indices from Deuteronomistic characteristics. When Deuteronomic words or phrases appear without Deuteronomistic indicators, he interprets them as either the result of the influential Josianic reform or as evidence of borrowing from the pages of the prophets and/or Baruch. With respect to style, the Deuteronomistic redactor shows a clear preference for conditional constructions and has often introduced alternatives into his speeches (something Herrmann had already observed and associated with Deuteronomistic ideology, as we have seen). Thiel describes this form as an "alternative sermon," a sermon which imagined viable options for the pre-exilic community—which had already sealed its fate with its choice—which were real options for those listening during the exile.

The Dtr redactor of Jeremiah transformed the materials at his disposal into editorial units (*redaktionelle Einheiten*) with two far-reaching concerns of the exilic community in mind. First, he was concerned with explaining the "*Unheil*" which befell Judah and Jerusalem in a conventionally acceptable and meaningful way. He did so by asserting that the event of 587 B.C.E. was God's judgment for the sins of his people.[71] The people of Judah had thus brought the disaster upon themselves. The second problem which the redactor addressed involved the future existence of the people of God. Could God's sentence of judgment be reversed? He responded to this anxiety by formulating a promise of salvation, namely, that the "history" of God with Israel had not come to an end but instead would begin anew on a radically improved basis at a future time. Thus the Deuteronomistic redactor helped eliminate the fear that the saving-history of God with Judah had come to an end.

In the approaches mentioned thus far, the prose sermons have been understood as expansion or recasting of the Jeremianic tradition in a subsequent period for a different situation under the direct influence of Deuteronomistic thought. As we have seen, the majority would now regard the time as the exilic period, the situation as that of the exiles in Babylon, and the association with Dtr in particular. Meanwhile other possible approaches to the prose sermons have been explored. In general these have been more concerned to explain the correspondences with Deuteronomistic tradition than to elaborate them, but they have often provided useful summaries of the data. These proposals have differed considerably among themselves, but taken together the basic argument they make is the following: that the resemblance to Dtr and Deuteronomy which has

---

[71]Thiel, *Die deuteronomistische Redaktion, 26-45*, p. 107.

been noted and understood to be evidence of redaction (1) can be accounted for equally well in other ways, and (2) cannot be properly interpreted without also considering (a) other distinctive features of the prose sermons which they do not share with Dtr or Deuteronomy, (b) many points of contact with undisputed prophecies of Jeremiah, and (c) instances where the prose sermons employ Dtr clichés and motifs in ways which are contrary, or even contradictory, to the sense they have in Dtr.

With regard to the first point, it has been suggested that Jeremiah himself employed (or was influenced directly by) Deuteronomic style and vocabulary in his oracular speeches. Accordingly, some critics claim that the advent of Deuteronomy and the influential nature of the Deutero-nomic reformation under Josiah in the seventh century led to Jeremiah's utilization of Deuteronomic style and language.[72] Somewhat differently, Oesterley and Robinson, as well as W. F. Albright and J. Bright (in a modified form), posited that the (Deuteronomic) literary style which emerges in the prose sermons of the book of Jeremiah as well as in Deu-teronomy reflects the form which Hebrew rhetorical prose took in the late seventh and early sixth centuries.[73] Similarly, Eissfeldt contended that the Jeremianic addresses, although indeed reminiscent of the diction and style of Deuteronomy and the Deuteronomists, actually reflect a form of speech which became increasingly prevalent in the beginning of the seventh century in priestly and prophetic circles.[74] A. Weiser argued that the Deuteronomistic style of the prose discourses is derived from the covenant tradition associated with the Jerusalem temple and its liturgy.[75] Likewise, J. W. Miller sought to explain the linguistic and stylistic

---

[72]For example, S. R. Driver, *Deuteronomy* (Edinburgh: T & T Clark, 1895), pp. xciiff.; Y. Kaufmann, *The Religion of Israel* (New York: Schocken, 1972), p. 415.

[73]W. O. E. Oesterley and Th. H. Robinson, *Introduction to the Books of the Old Testament* (London, 1934); John Bright, "The Date of the Prose Sermons of Jeremiah," *Journal of Biblical Literature* 70 (1951) 15-35; W. F. Albright, "A Supplement of Jeremiah: The Lachish Ostraca," *Bulletin of the American Schools of Oriental Research* 61 (1936) : 14f.; "A Reexamination of the Lachish Letters," *Bulletin of the American Schools of Oriental Research* 73 (1939) : 20.

[74]Otto Eissfeldt, *The Old Testament. An Introduction*, trans. P. R. Ackroyd (New York: Harper & Row, 1976), pp. 15f., 352.

[75]Artur Weiser, *Das Buch des Propheten Jeremia,* Das Alte Testament Deutsche, 20-21, 4th ed. (Göttingen: Vandenhoeck and Ruprecht, 1960).

similarities between the prose sermons in Jeremiah and the Deuteronomistic literary corpus by suggesting that both blocks of material employed
a common liturgical *Gattung* whose *Sitz im Leben* was the Jerusalem
Temple.[76] Robert R. Wilson has argued recently that Jeremiah, as a
member of one of the priestly groups that carried the old Ephraimite
traditions, employed the stereotyped language, speech patterns, and
theology (of Deuteronomy) expected by his support group, the Ephraimite
priests at Anathoth.[77]

The second point may be stated simply as follows: although the prose
sermons in Jeremiah are similar to the Deuteronomistic literary corpus,
they nevertheless enjoy a style and diction of their own and thus are to be
reckoned as part of the authentic Jeremianic tradition. This thesis has
been couched in several ways. In his important article of 1951,[78] John
Bright drew up a list of expressions characteristic of the prose sermons in
Jeremiah. He used this table to argue that these materials, although
admittedly close to Dtr in both style and idea, reflect their own distinctive style and ideology and are "by no means a slavish imitation of it."[79]
Moreover, the language employed in these discourses has many points of
contact with that of the poetic oracles of the prophet. This observation
led Bright to suspect "a definite kinship between the prose sermons and
the genuine Jeremiah . . . ."[80]

Bright's suggestion was taken up by W. L. Holladay, who argued in his
article "Prototype and Copies: A New Approach to the Poetry-Prose
Problem in the Book of Jeremiah"[81] that many of the prose phrases in the
Jeremianic addresses represent "prosaicized copies of prototype phrases
found in Jeremiah's poetry or in other prophetic poetry, or in some cases
in other earlier traditional lore."[82] Holladay drew the conclusion that the
style of the prose sermons as a whole cannot properly be identified as

---

[76]J. W. Miller, *Das Verhältnis Jeremias und Hesekiels sprachlich und
theologisch untersucht* (Assen: Van Gorcum, 1955).

[77]Robert Wilson, *Prophecy and Society in Ancient Israel* (Philadelphia:
Fortress, 1980), pp. 233ff.

[78]Bright, "Prose Sermons."

[79]Ibid., p. 26.

[80]Ibid.

[81]W. L. Holladay, "Prototype and Copies: A New Approach to the
Poetry-Prose Problem in the Book of Jeremiah," *Journal of Biblical Literature* 79 (1960) : 351-67.

[82]W. L. Holladay, "A Fresh Look at 'Source B' and 'Source C' in Jeremiah," *Vetus Testamentum* 25 (1975) : 402.

Deuteronomic. Instead, they represent "Baruch's adaptation of Jeremiah's poetic message."[83]

Helga Weippert went a step further than Holladay in her contention that many of the prose discourses in the book of Jeremiah are not prose but rather *Kunstprosa* (artistic/formal prose). According to Weippert, this artistic prose, which is characterized by irregular parallelism of thought and extended word-groups, has its origin in poetry.[84] Although she admits that this demetrification of the prophetic word occurs in Dtr (e.g., 1 Sam 12:7-25; 1 Kgs 8:1-14ff.) as well as in the addresses in the Jeremiah book, Weippert argues that the two have a common origin in the poetic literature. Owing to this and other observations (see below), she maintains that the "prose" discourses are not from the hand of a later Deuteronomistic redactor but from the prophet himself.[85]

Lastly, it has been argued that many of the ideas which find expression in the prose sermons in the book of Jeremiah run counter to the general direction of Deuteronomy and the Deuteronomistic historical work and conform instead to the indisputably authentic Jeremianic oracles. The most recent and perhaps best representative of this line of reasoning is H. Weippert. Weippert's basic contention is that "it is the context which defines and determines the distinctive meaning of a word or formula employed by a particular writer as opposed to other possible meanings in other contexts."[86] On the basis of this principle, she examines four extended discourses and a number of words and phrases in five shorter passages, all of which have been commonly assigned to a Deuteronomistic hand, and concludes that these materials are closer to the authentic block of tradition in the book of Jeremiah than to the Deuteronomistic literary corpus. As a result of her contextual analysis of the alleged Dtr phrases occurring in the prose addresses, Weippert finds that these words and phrases are often employed in ways which directly contradict their usage and meaning in Dtr literature. From her exegesis of Jer 7:1-15, 18:1-12, 21:1-7 and 34:8-22 she draws the conclusion that the parenetic sections of

---

[83]Ibid.

[84]Helga Weippert, *Die Prosareden des Jeremiabuches* (Berlin: Walter de Gruyter, 1973), p. 78.

[85]Ibid., pp. 228ff. Weippert qualifies this statement by contending: "Hier bleibt ein weiter Raum für die Einzelanalyse, die von Fall zu Fall entscheiden muss, ob ein Prosaabschnitt von Jeremia stammt oder nicht. . . . Im Falle von Jer 17:19-27 ist etwa eine Zurückführung auf Jeremia problematisch" (p. 234).

[86]Ibid., p. 24.

these passages are entirely consistent with the prophet's promulgation of Yahweh's word in A sections and thus should not be treated as secondary, unauthentic accretions.[87]

These studies illustrate the basic areas of disagreement in current research. Although sharply expressed, they are in fact narrow in scope, and there are broad areas of agreement as well. It is now generally acknowledged that the writings ascribed to C sections were composed on the basis of authentic Jeremianic material, even though there is still a difference of opinion about how much it has been recast in the process. Moreover, numerous linguistic, formal and theological points of contact with Deuteronomistic literature are recognized and these are regarded as characteristic indices of C materials as a whole. It is also generally agreed that the points of correspondence between Dtr and the prose sermons are significantly greater than those existing between Dtr and other prophetic writings of the exilic period (e.g., Ezekiel, Isa 40-55).

The areas of disagreement are a reminder that the available evidence is limited. Taken altogether, the literature surviving from this period does not allow us to identify with certainty a Hebrew rhetorical prose typical of the late seventh to mid-sixth centuries, or to identify and distinguish all the coherent groups of that period which might have influenced the prophet or those who handed on his words. Furthermore, the Deuteronomistic tradition itself must be regarded as a trajectory rather than a fixed point; it must have been constantly changing and developing throughout this period, however slowly.[88] This being so, it remains a possibility that

---

[87]Ibid., pp. 232f.

[88]Moshe Weinfeld, for example, has emphasized that Deuteronomistic tradition was not a static school of thought but one which underwent a formative process and historical development. Accordingly, those responsible for the Jeremianic prose sermons did not merely emulate the diction of Deuteronomy and Dtr—an assumption shared by the overwhelming majority of scholars—but developed generally conventional expressions by giving them a more specific sense. Thus the prose discourses in Jeremiah represent a new stage in the historical development of the Deuteronomistic school. The course of the formation and historical development is described by Weinfeld in the following way:

1. The book of Deuteronomy, composed in the latter half of the seventh century;
2. The Deuteronomistic edition of Joshua-Kings, which received its fixed form in the first half of the sixth century;
3. The Deuteronomistic prose sermons in Jeremiah, which were

the prose sermons developed fully within this tradition even if they differ on occasion from Dtr. In any event, correspondences between the prose sermons and the undisputed Jeremianic materials are not conclusive evidence that the sermons derive from the prophet himself; they indicate only that those who composed the sermons (whoever they may have been) knew the Jeremianic tradition and employed it.

A CATALOG OF WORDS AND PHRASES

As our brief survey has shown, scholars have appealed primarily to linguistic data. Although theological, stylistic, and formal/structural considerations are no less important, these have for the most part been employed secondarily, in conjunction with linguistic analysis. This admittedly lopsided emphasis on language data is no doubt due, at least in part, to the fact that such analyses are easier to categorize and control. Here we are dealing with discrete observations which are easily stated and enumerated, and we need only bring together in a single list the contributions of many scholars from the nineteenth century to the present.

In the nineteenth century, Leopold Zunz, John Colenso, and S. R. Driver prepared tables which were primarily intended to clarify the relationship between the book of Jeremiah and Deuteronomy.[89] Driver's table is more helpful than those of Zunz and Colenso since, in addition to linguistic parallels between Jeremiah and Deuteronomy, he entered the most noticeable words and phrases occurring in Deuteronomistic literature in general. The early twentieth century produced one of the most comprehensive tabulations of stereotyped expressions in Jeremiah, in Hölscher's *Die Profeten*.[90] Hölscher's list included many phrases which occur rarely in the prose sermons, however, which makes it less useful for our purposes, and he did not differentiate prose and poetry. H. G. May tabulated forty-one examples of the diction employed by "Jeremiah's

---

apparently composed during the second half of the sixth century. See his *Deuteronomy and the Deuteronomic School* (Oxford: Clarendon Press, 1972), pp. 6ff.

[89]Leopold Zunz, *Zeitschrift der Morgenländischen Gesellschaft* (1873), pp. 670-73; John Colenso, *The Pentateuch and the Book of Joshua Critically Examined*, part 7, appendix 149 (1879); S. R. Driver, *A Critical and Exegetical Commentary on Deuteronomy* (1895), pp. lxxviii-lxxxiii, xciii-xcv.

[90]Hölscher, *Die Profeten*, pp. 382-84.

biographer."[91] His list is pertinent to the present discussion only insofar as his data pertains directly to Deuteronomistic literature. May's "biographer," who was active not earlier than the first half of the fifth century B.C.E., is not a Deuteronomic or Deuteronomistic redactor/editor, but an individual influenced by D^2, 2 Isaiah, 1 Zechariah, and the editor of Ezekiel.[92] In his "The Date of the Prose Sermons of Jeremiah,"[93] John Bright collated expressions characteristic of the Jeremianic prose sermons, together with linguistic parallels outside Jeremiah, particularly in Dtr literature. Although Bright's table is not comprehensive, it is very helpful in that his controls are tighter than those of previous lists, and his tabulation of typical prose phrases includes parallels from the Deuteronomic literary corpus. The most recent as well as most comprehensive table of linguistic indices of the C material in Jeremiah has been presented by Moshe Weinfeld in his *Deuteronomy and the Deuteronomic School.* His tabulation of Deuteronomic phrases occurring in the Jeremianic prose addresses is divided into ten theological and stylistic categories, under which appropriate phrases are listed.

In the table of linguistic indices proposed below, we have divided the data into the four categories referred to in chapter I. Category I includes only words and phrases attested more than once in the Deuteronomistic historical work (Dtr). Category II includes words and phrases which occur only once in Dtr. Category III comprises diction found in Deuteronomy proper (Dt = 4:44-29:1) but not in Dtr. Category IV lists words and phrases which are not attested in Dt or Dtr but which have been said to resemble their diction. All the idioms referred to by more than one scholar as indicative of C's provenience and its association with Deuteronomic and/or Deuteronomistic tradition are included in these lists, even though some of those listed in categories I, II and III appear in the C corpus only once. All the words and phrases listed in category IV appear in the C corpus two times or more.

---

[91]H. G. May, "Towards an Objective Approach to the Book of Jeremiah: The Biographer," *Journal of Biblical Literature* 61 (1942) : 154f.

[92]Ibid., pp. 147ff.

[93]Bright, "Prose Sermons," pp. 30-35.

I. C Diction Attested More than Once in Dtr

1. שמעו בקולי

"obey/hearken to my voice"
Dtr: high incidence in Dtr and Dt (more than 40 times)
Jer C: 3:13; 7:23; 28; 11:4, 7; 18:10; 32:23; 35:8

2. יצא/עלה אבותיכם . . . מארץ מצרים

"I/who brought you/your fathers out of the land of Egypt"
Dtr: fairly high incidence in Dtr and Dt (ca. 20 times)
Jer C: 7:22, 25; 11:4, 7; 16:14, 15; 34:13; cf. 31:32; 32:21

3. הלך אחרי אלהים אחרים

"to go after other gods"
Dtr: Judg 2:12, 19; 1 Kgs 11:10 (and attested frequently in Deut)
Jer C: 7:6, 9; 11:10; 16:11; 25:6; 35:15

4. הארץ/המקום . . . אשר נתתי לכם/לאבותיכם

"the land/place/city/inheritance which I gave to you/your fathers/
them"
Dtr: Deut 3:19, 20; 1 Kgs 9:7; 2 Kgs 21:8
Jer C: 7:7, 14; 16:15; 25:5; 35:15; cf. 11:5; 24:10; 30:3

5. עבדי/ו הנביאים

"my/his servants the prophets"
Dtr: 2 Kgs 17:13, 23; 21:10; 24:2
Jer C: 7:25; 25:4; 29:19; 35:15; 44:4

6. עבד אתם/עבד אלהים אחרים

"to serve other gods/to serve them (i.e., other gods)"
Dtr: Josh 23:16; 1 Sam 8:8; 1 Kgs 9:6; cf. 2 Kgs 21:21
Jer C: 16:11, 13; 25:6; 35:15; 44:3

7. למען הכעסני

"to provoke me to anger"
Dtr: 1 Kgs 14:9; 16:2; 2 Kgs 22:17
Jer C: 7:18; 32:29, 32; 44:3; cf. 11:17

8. ‏למען/להכעסי במעשה ידיכם‎
   "to provoke me/him with the work of your/their hands"
   Dtr: Deut 31:29; 1 Kgs 16:7; 2 Kgs 22:17
   Jer C: 25:6, 7; 32:30; 44:8

9. ‏עשה הרע/הישר בעיני יהוה‎
   "to do that which is evil/right in the sight of Yahweh"
   Dtr: high incidence in Dtr and Dt (more than 50 times)
   Jer C: 7:30; 18:10; 32:30; 34:15

10. ‏הנני/הנה אנכי מביא על . . .‎
    "behold, I am bringing evil upon . . ."
    Dtr: 1 Kgs 14:10; 21:21; 2 Kgs 21:12; 22:16; cf. 1 Kgs 9:9; 21:29;
    2 Kgs 22:20
    Jer C: 11:11; 19:3; 35:17; 45:5; cf. 19:15; 39:16

11. ‏כל ממלכות ארץ‎
    "all the kingdoms of the earth"
    Dtr: 2 Kgs 19:15, 19 (=Isa 37:16, 20); cf. Deut 28:25
    Jer C: 29:18; 34:1, 17; cf. 15:4; 24:9; 25:26

12. ‏שוב איש מדרכו הרעה‎
    "to turn from his evil way"
    Dtr: 1 Kgs 13:33; 2 Kgs 17:13
    Jer C: 18:11; 25:5; 35:15; cf. 26:3; 36:3, 7

13. ‏שפך/מלא דם נקי‎
    "to shed/pour innocent blood"
    Dtr: 2 Kgs 21:16; 24:4; cf. Deut 19:10, 13: 21:8
    Jer C: 7:6; 19:4; 22:3

14. ‏כיום הזה‎
    "as at this day"
    Dtr: Deut 2:30; 3:6; 4:20
    Jer C: 11:5; 32:20; 44:6; cf. 25:18; 44:22, 23

15. ‏הקים דבר יהוה‎
    "to establish the word of Yahweh (as fulfillment of prophecy)
    Dtr: 1 Kgs 2:4; 8:20; 12:15; cf. Deut 9:5; 1 Kgs 6:12
    Jer C: 29:10; 33:14

16. ארץ זבת חלב ודבש
"a land flowing with milk and honey"
Dtr: Deut 31:20; Josh 5:6; cf. Deut 6:3; 11:9; passim
Jer C: 11:5; 32:22

17. בכל-לבה
"with all the heart"
Dtr: 1 Sam 12:20, 24; 1 Kgs 8:23; 14:8; 2 Kgs 10:31
Jer C: 3:10; 29:13; cf. 24:7

18. יד חזקה וזרע נטויה
"a strong hand and outstretched arm"
Dtr: Deut 4:34; 1 Kgs 8:42
Jer C: 21:5 (inverted order); 32:21

19. שקוצים
"detestable things" (referring to idolatry)
Dtr: 1 Kgs 11:5, 7; 2 Kgs 23:24; cf. Deut 29:16
Jer C: 7:30; 32:34

20. תועבה
"abomination" (referring to idolatry)
Dtr: 1 Kgs 14:24; 2 Kgs 16:3; 21:2, 11
Jer C: 32:35; 44:4; cf. 16:18; 44:22

21. למען ייטב לכם
"that it may be well with you/them"
Dtr: Deut 4:40; 2 Kgs 25:24; cf. Deut 5:16; 6:3; passim
Jer C: 7:23; cf. 38:20; 40:9; 42:6

22. בכל לב ובכל נפש
"with all your/the heart and all your/the soul"
Dtr: Deut 4:29; Josh 22:5; 23:14; 1 Kgs 2:4; 8:23; 2 Kgs 23:3, 25
Jer C: 32:41 (a reference to Yahweh's attitude towards his people)

23. על-כל-הר גבה ואל-תחת כל-עץ רענן
"on (every) mountain and under every luxuriant tree"
Dtr: 1 Kgs 14:23; 2 Kgs 16:4; 17:10; cf. Deut 12:2
Jer C: 3:6; cf. 2:20; 17:2

24. ‏מכור הברזל‏
    "from the iron-furnace"
    Dtr: Deut 4:20; 1 Kgs 8:51
    Jer C: 11:4

25. ‏ירא את יהוה (כל הימים/כל ימי חייך)‏
    "to fear Yahweh (as long as you live)"
    Dtr: Deut 4:10; 31:12, 13; Josh 4:24; 1 Sam 12:14, 24; 1 Kgs 8:40,
    43; 2 Kgs 17:32, 33, 34, passim
    Jer C: 32:39

26. ‏החטיא את ישראל/הארץ/יהודה‏
    "to cause Israel/the land/Judah to sin"
    Dtr: widely attested in Dtr (ca. 18 times)
    Jer C: 32:35

27. ‏סור מאחרי יהוה‏
    "to turn (away) from Yahweh"
    Dtr: 1 Sam 12:20; 2 Kgs 18:6
    Jer C: 32:40

28. ‏שוב אל יהוה בכל לב‏
    "to return to Yahweh with all the heart"
    Dtr: 1 Kgs 8:48; 2 Kgs 23:25
    Jer C: 3:10; cf. 24:7

29. ‏הלך בכל הדרך/בכל דרכיו‏
    "to walk in all his way(s)"
    Dtr: Josh 22:5; 1 Kgs 8:58; 2 Kgs 21:21
    Jer C: 7:23

30. ‏(מכעיסים) מן היום אשר יצאו ממצרים ועד היום הזה‏
    "(to rebel/vex) from the day that you/they left Egypt until this
    day"
    Dtr: 1 Sam 8:8; 2 Kgs 21:15; cf. Deut 9:7
    Jer C: 7:25; cf. 32:31

31. בחר
"to choose" (Israel; with reference to its election as Yahweh's covenant people)
Dtr: Deut 4:37 1 Kgs 3:8; cf. Deut 7:6, 7; 10:15; 14:2
Jer C: 33:24

32. לא יכרת לך איש מעל כסא ישראל
"there shall not be cut off a man from you from the throne of Israel"
Dtr: 1 Kgs 2:4; 8:25; 9:5
Jer C: 33:17; cf. 33:18; 35:19

33. השלך מעל פני יהוה
"to cast away from before the face/presence of Yahweh"
Dtr: 2 Kgs 13:23; 17:20; 24:20 (=Jer 52:3)
Jer C: 7:15

34. הסיר מעל פני יהוה
"to remove from before the face/presence of Yahweh"
Dtr: 2 Kgs 17:18, 23; 23:27; 24:3
Jer C: 32:31

35. בא וירש את הארץ
"to enter and possess the land/it"
Dtr: Deut 4:1, 5; Josh 1:11; 18:3
Jer C: 32:23

36. השמרו ב/לנפשותיכם
"watch your soul(s)"
Dtr: Deut 4:15; Josh 23:11; cf. Deut 4:9
Jer C: 17:21

37. עמך ישראל
"thy people Israel" (as a liturgical term)
Dtr: 2 Sam 7:23, 24; 1 Kgs 8:33, 34, 38, 43, 52
Jer C: 32:21

II. C Diction Attested Once in Dtr

38. ‏קטר אלהים אחרים/לבעל‏
"to burn incense to foreign gods/to Baal"
Dtr: 2 Kgs 22:17; cf. 2 Kgs 17:16; 21:3, 5; 23:5
Jer C: 7:9; 11:12, 13; 19:4; 32:29; 44:3, 5, 8; cf. 44:15

39. ‏נתן/היה לשמה שרקה חרבה חרפה . . . (בכל העמים)‏
"to become an astonishment, desolation, hiss, reproach, curse,
proverb, and byword (to all the nations)"
Dtr: 2 Kgs 22:19; cf. Deut 28:25, 37
Jer C: 19:8; 25:9, 11; 27:17; 29:18; 44:6, 8, 12; cf. 24:9; 25:18;
26:6; 42:18; frequently found in series of two or more

40. ‏אשר נקרא שמי עליו‏
"which is called by my name"
Dtr: 1 Kgs 8:43; cf. Deut 28:10
Jer C: 7:10, 11, 14, 30; 32:34; 34:15

41. ‏איש יהודה וישבי ירושלם‏
"the men of Judah and the inhabitants of Jerusalem"
Dtr: 2 Kgs 23:2 (=II Chron 34:30)
Jer C: 11:2, 9; 17:25; 18:11; 32:32; 35:13

42. ‏דברי הברית‏
"the words of the covenant"
Dtr 2 Kgs 23:3; cf. Deut 29:1, 9
Jer C: 11:2, 3, 6, 8; 34:18

43. ‏הנה ימים באים‏
"behold, days are coming"
Dtr: 1 Sam 2:31 (elsewhere 2 Kgs 20:17; Amos 4:2; 8:11; 9:13)
Jer C: 7:32; 16:14; 19:6; 33:14; cf. 23:5, 7; 30:3; 31:27, 31, 38;
48:12; 49:2; 51:47, 52

44. ‏היה לי לעם‏
"to be his people"
Dtr: Deut 4:20; cf. Deut 7:6; 14:2; 26:18; 27:9
Jer C: 7:23; 11:4; 32:38; cf. 24:7; 30:22, 25; 31:32

45. הלך בתורת יהוה
"to walk in the law of Yahweh"
Dtr: 2 Kgs 10:31
Jer C: 32:23; 44:10; cf. 26:4; 44:23

46. הקשה עורף
"to stiffen the neck"
Dtr: 2 Kgs 17:14; cf. Deut 10:16
Jer C: 7:25; 17:23; cf. 19:15

47. לדמן על פני האדמה
"(the corpse) shall be dung on the face of the earth"
Dtr: 2 Kgs 9:37
Jer C: 8:2; 16:4; cf. 25:33

48. רנה ותפלה
"cry/exultation and prayer"
Dtr: 1 Kgs 8:28
Jer C: 7:16; 11:14

49. אשר כל שמעה תצלנה שתי אזניו
"so that whoever hears it, his ears shall tingle"
Dtr: 2 Kgs. 21:12; cf. 1 Sam 3:11
Jer C: 19:3

50. בכח גדול ובזרע נטויה
"with great might and an outstretched arm"
Dtr: 2 Kgs 17:36; cf. Deut 9:29
Jer C: 32:17; cf. 27:5

III. C Diction Unattested in Dtr but Attested in Deuteronomy

51. שוב (H) את שבות . . . .
"to restore the fortunes of . . ."
Dt: 30:3
Jer C: 29:14; 32:44; 33:7, 11, 26; cf. 30:3; 31:23

52. אשר הדחתי שם
"to be driven there" (as punishment)
Dt: 30:1, 3
Jer C: 8:3; 16:15; 29:14, 18; 32:37; cf. 24:9; 27:10, 15

53. והיתה נבלתך למאכל לעוף השמים ולבהמת הארץ
"your corpse shall be food for the birds of the heaven and beasts
of the earth"
Dt: 28:26; cf. 1 Kgs 14:11; 16:4; 21:24; 2 Kgs 9:37
Jer C: 7:33; 16:4; 19:7; 34:20

54. הלך בשרירות לב/אחרי שרירות לב
"to walk in/after the stubbornness of the heart"
Dt: 29:18
Jer C: 7:24; 11:8; 16:12; cf. 18:12

55. (אלהים אחרים) אשר לא ידעתם
"(other gods) whom you/they have not known"
Dt: 11:28; 13:3, 7, 14; 28:64; 29:25
Jer C: 7:9; 19:4; 44:3; cf. 9:16; 16:13; passim

56. נתן/היה לזעוה לכל ממלכות הארץ
"to become a horror to all the kingdoms of the earth"
Dt: 28:25
Jer C: 29:18; 34:17; cf. 15:4; 24:9

57. באף ובחמה ובקצף גדול
"with anger, fury, and great wrath"
Dt: 29:27
Jer C: 21:5; 32:37

58. גר יתום ואלמנה
"stranger, orphan and widow" (as types of the socially deprived)
Dt: 10:18; 24:17, 19, 20, 21; 27:19; passim
Jer C: 7:6; 22:3

59. בית עבדים
"the house of bondage"
Dt: 5:6; 6:12; 7:8; 8:14; 13:6, 11
Jer C: 34:13

60. ואמרו אליך על מה דבר/עשה יהוה . . . ואמרו (אליהם) על
. . . אשר עזבו אותי/ברית יהוה . . .
". . . and they will say/ask 'why has Yahweh done . . . ?' And they
will reply: 'Because they have forsaken the covenant of Yahweh'"
Dt: 29:23f.; cf. 1 Kgs 9:8-9b.
Jer C: 16:10f.; cf. 5:19; 9:11f.; 22:8f.

61. שוש עליהם להטיב
"to rejoice over you/them in making you/them prosperous"
Dt: 28:63; 30:9
Jer C: 32:41

62. האכיל את בשר בניהם ואת בשר בנתיהם
"to make them eat the flesh of their sons and the flesh of their
daughters . . ."
Dt: 28:53
Jer C: 19:9

63. מרע מעלליכם
"because of the evil of their doings"
Dt: 28:20; cf. Isa 1:16; Hos 9:15; Ps 28:4
Jer C: 25:5; cf. 26:3; 44:22

64. נתן לפניך החיים והמות
"to set before you . . . life and death"
Dt: 30:15, 19
Jer C: 21:8

65. ארור האיש אשר לא ישמע/יקים את דברי הברית/התורה הזאת
"cursed (be) the man who shall not hearken/establish the words of
this covenant/torah"
Dt: 27:26
Jer C: 11:3

66. השבועה אשר נשבעתי לאבותיכם
"the oath which I/he swore to your fathers . . . "
Dt: 7:8; cf. Deut 8:18, 9:5
Jer C: 11:5

67. ‏(המקום אשר יבחר) לשכן שמו שם‏
"(the site that Yahweh will choose) to make his name dwell there"
Dt: 12:11; 14:23; 16:2, 6, 11; cf. 1 Kgs 9:3; 11:36; 14:21; 2 Kgs
21:4, 7
Jer C: 7:12

IV. Other Common C Diction

68. ‏יהוה צבאות אלהי ישראל‏
"Yahweh of hosts, God of Israel"
Jer C: very frequent (ca. 20 times); 7:3, 21; 16:9; 19:3; 27:4, 21;
29:4, 8, 21, 25; 32:14, 15; 35:13, 17, 18, 19; 39:16; 44:2, 7, 11

69. ‏חרב רעב דבר‏
"sword, famine, and pestilence"
Jer C: 16:4 (in part); 21:7, 9; 27:8, 13; 29:17, 18; 32:24, 36; 34:17;
44:12 (twice), 13; cf. 24:10; 42:17, 22: 44:27; 1 Kgs 8:37; 2 Sam
24:13

70. ‏השכם ודבר/ושלח‏ . . .
"rising up early and . . . " (an infinitive)
Jer C: 7:13, 25; 11:7; 25:3, 4; 29:19; 32:33; 35:14, 15; 44:4

71. ‏הדבר אשר היה אל ירמיהו מאת יהוה‏
"the word which came (lit. was) to Jeremiah from Yahweh"
Jer C: 7:1; 11:1; 18:1; 21:1; 27:1; 32:1; 34:1, 8; 35:1; cf. 25:1; 30:1;
40:1; 44:1

72. ‏ולא הטו את אזנם‏
"they did not incline the ear"
Jer C: 7:24, 26; 11:8; 17:23; 25:4; 34:14; 35:15; 44:5; cf. 2 Kgs
19:16

73. ‏אדם ובהמה‏
"man and beast"
Jer C: 7:20; 21:6; 27:5; 32:43; 33:10 (twice), 12; cf. 31:27; 36:29;
51:62

74. ‏בערי יהודה ובחוצות ירושלם‏
"the cities of Judah and the streets of Jerusalem"
Jer C: 7:17, 34; 11:6; 33:10; 44:6; cf. 17:21

75. נבא שקר
"to prophesy lies"
Jer C: 27:10, 14, 16; 29:9, 21; cf. 23:25, 26, 32, 29:23; 40:16; 43:2

76. פקד על . . .
"to punish/visit upon"
Jer C: 25:12; 27:8, 29:32; 44:13 (twice); cf. 9:24, 15:3, 23:2, 34; 44:29

77. מבקשי נפשם
"they that seek life"
Jer C: 19:7, 9; 21:7; 34:20, 21; cf. 11:21; 22:25; 38:16; 44:30

78. קול ששון וקול שמחה קול חתן וקול כלה
"the voice of mirth and the voice of gladness, the voice of the bridegroom and the voice of the bride"
Jer C: 7:34; 16:9; 25:10; 33:11

79. לקח מוקר
"to receive correction/discipline"
Jer C: 7:28; 17:23; 32:33; 35:13

80. נביאיכם . . .
"your/their prophets"
Jer C: 27:9, 16; 29:8; 32:32; cf. 37:19

81. עבד ב . . .
"to make bondmen of . . ." (referring exclusively to persons)
Jer C: 25:14; 27:7; 34:9, 10; cf. 30:8

82. היטיבו דרכיכם ומעלליכם
"amend your ways and your doings"
Jer C: 7:3, 5; 18:11; 35:15 (in part); cf. 26:13

83. הבאים בשערים האלה
"that enter these gates"
Jer C: 7:2; 17:20; 19:3 (attested in the OG only); 22:2

84. אשר לא צויתי ולא עלתה על לבי
"which I did not command nor did it even enter my mind"
Jer C: 7:31; 19:5; 32:35

85. לא יאקפו ולא יקברו/ולא יקפדו להם
   "they shall not be gathered, nor buried/lamented"
   Jer C: 8:2; 16:4, 6; cf. 25:33

86. לבנות ולנטוע . . .
   "to build and plant, pull down and uproot" (i.e., the contrasting
   ideas in the verbs)
   Jer C: 18:7, 9; 45:4; cf. 1:10; 24:6; 31:28; 42:10

87. בטח לשקר/על דברי השקר
   "to trust in lying words/a lie"
   Jer C: 7:4, 8; 29:31; cf. 28:15

88. מלכים שרים כהנים ונביאים . . .
   "kings, princes, priests, prophets, etc." (or similarly)
   Jer C: 8:1; 17:25; 32:32; cf. 1:18; 2:26; 13:13; 44:17, 21

89. קרא ולא ענה
   "to call . . . but not to answer"
   Jer C: 7:13, 27; 35:17

90. נבוכדראצר עבדי
   "Nebuchadnezzar, my servant" (i.e., Yahweh's servant)
   Jer C: 25:9; 27:6; 43:10

91. הרעה אשר דבר על . . .
   "the evil that he pronounced/spoke against you"
   Jer C: 18:8; 35:17; cf. 19:15

92. מלכים (ושרים) ישבים על כסא דוד רכבים ברכב ובסוסים
   "kings (and princes) sitting upon the throne of David riding in
   chariots and on horses"
   Jer C: 17:25; 22:4

A Résumé of Other Indices

As we turn now to other indices, we move from individual words and
phrases to larger literary units and even to observations about the corpus
as a whole. These cannot be catalogued in precisely the same way as the

linguistic indices above. Instead we shall offer a résumé of what scholars have said about these matters.

With respect to style, C has been said to show a marked tendency to use a limited number of words in a highly repetitious, monotonous and prolix manner. Its sermonic style is rhetorical in nature and parenetic in tone. C's homilies often employ conventional formulae and phraseology and thus lack the creative imagination and richness of ideas found in the poetic Jeremianic oracles. Notwithstanding, its prose style and general tone of admonition exhibit a simplicity and candor which help drive home the prophetic message with great force.

Although Mowinckel had observed that many C sermons exhibit a structure which includes a summons to repentance and conversion, a description of the people's wrongdoing, and a statement regarding the result of the wrongdoing, namely judgment, it was primarily the achievement of Janssen and Nicholson to advance form-critical arguments for a Deuteronomistic provenience of the C corpus. Janssen affirmed that several speeches in Jeremiah and the Deuteronomistic historical work follow the same conventional form: an introduction, a recital of Yahweh's words and/or acts, a description of disobedience, and a statement of the imminent threats or promises.[94] Based primarily on the work of D. J. McCarthy's *Treaty and Covenant*,[95] Nicholson identified this structure more precisely as the covenant form reminiscent of the ancient Near Eastern vassal treaties.[96]

As for the theological features characteristic of the C material, many scholars have held that its representation of the prophet's role and function is essentially Deuteronomic in outlook and thus markedly different from the conception of the prophet in the undisputed Jeremianic tradition. The following résumé consists of those particular features most commonly regarded as indicative of this.

1) In the prose sermons the prophets, including Jeremiah himself, constitute an institutional succession of inspired spokesmen and preachers of the Law. Moses is depicted as the prophet *par excellence* of this prophetic line (Dtr: 1 Kgs 11:30ff.; 14:7ff.; 16:1ff.; passim; 2 Kgs 17:13f.; Jer C: 7:13-18; 25:4-11; 29:17-19; 44:4-6; passim).

---

[94]See pp. 20-22 above.

[95]D. J. McCarthy, *Treaty and Covenant*, Analecta Biblica 21 (Rome, 1963).

[96]Nicholson, *Preaching*, pp. 32f.

2) In accordance with Dtr ideas, the primary function of these spokesmen is to warn the people of God of the consequences of rebellion and disobedience to the Law. They are concerned foremost with Israel's obedience to the commandments given by Moses in the form of Deut.

3) The Deuteronomistic message of the prophets which finds expression in the C corpus may be summarized as follows:

   a. Yahweh sends "his servants the prophets" to summon Israel to repent of its wrongdoing;
   b. Israel rejects the message of repentance spoken by the prophets;
   c. As a result of Israel's rebellion and rejection of the prophetic proclamation, which often takes the form of Deuteronomic dictates, Yahweh punishes his people (7:25-27, 32-34; 25:4-11; 29:17-19; cf. 35:15-17; 44:4-6).

4) Emulating the prophet *par excellence*, Moses, the prophet in C serves as a (covenant) intermediary between Yahweh and his people (Dtr/Dt: the portrayal of Moses in Deut takes the form of an intermediary through whom the Law was given to Israel at Horeb; Jer C: 7:16; 11:14; 16:5; 27:18).

The prose sermons and the Deuteronomistic historical work exhibit a fundamental concern over the *Unheil* which befell Judah in 587. Moreover, they attempt to come to terms with this perplexing historical reality in virtually identical ways (regardless of the fact that the C material and Dtr represent two different literary genres [i.e., prophecy and history]).

1) Both Dtr and Jer C assert that the tragic historical realities associated with the year 587 (and beyond) were the direct result of Yahweh's righteous judgment pronounced upon his covenant people for their disobedience to the words of Moses, as spoken in Deut and to the words of the prophets. Accordingly, the people of Judah brought the disaster upon themselves; Yahweh acted only in accordance with his revealed law (Dtr: Deut 4:25-27; Josh 23:16; 1 Sam 12:15, 25; 1 Kgs 9:6f.; 2 Kgs 17:19f.; Jer C: 7:13-15; 11:7-8; 16:10-13; 22:5; 25:8-13; 44:7-14).

2) In Dtr and in Jer C, idolatry, the worship of (foreign) deities other than Yahweh, is one of the gravest sins. The gravity of this particular sin is due to the fundamental importance given to the ideal of exclusive loyalty, devotion and allegiance to Yahweh in these two literary corpora (i.e., a strong anti-syncretistic tendency). In the book of Kings, for example, this Dtr *Tendenz* is manifested by the fact that a pure Yahwistic cult in Jerusalem became the main criterion by which to judge each king's success or failure in the sight of the deity. In the C material, the sins of the past and present people of God consist above all in their apostasy from Yahweh, which is thought of as virtually equivalent to idolatry.

Conversely, obedience to Yahweh's commandments is considered equal to exclusive loyalty and devotion to Yahweh (Dtr: 1 Kgs 9:8-9 and throughout the Deuteronomistic historical work; Jer C: 3:6-10; 7:16-18, 30f.; 16:10-11; 19:3-6; 25:5-7; 32:29, 34f.; 35:15; 44:3-5, 15-19, 24-25).

3) The incessant and obdurate nature of Judah's sins is a dominant motif in the prose discourse in Jeremiah, as well as a major theological index in Dtr. In a penetrating manner, these two literary corpora tell of the persistence and hard-heartedness of the covenant people's rebellion and disobedience; invariably the present people of God walk in the ways of their fathers and do that which is evil in the sight of Yahweh (Dtr: Deut 31:16-18; 1 Kgs 21:15; 2 Kgs 17:14-19; and passim; Jer C: 7:23-26, 27f.; 11:7-8; 16:11f.; 19:14f.; 25:3f., 7; 32:23, 30, 33; 44:9; passim).

4) A legalistic, peculiarly Deuteronomistic perception of the deity's will pervades the materials ascribed to the C tradition. According to Mowinckel, in the C materials the Law is perceived as a "fixed, written, and casuistically determined entity."[97] As Duhm put it: "Their theology is that of legalism, the Torah is their be-all and end-all."[98] Thus the ancestors as well as the contemporary people of God are accused of violating both the spirit of the Law and specific commandments set forth in the Law of Moses (11:3, 6; 17:19-27; 19:5-6; 34:8-12; 44:10).

The prose sermons in Jeremiah and Dtr are said to share a common theology of history, with special emphasis on the doctrine of retribution.

1) Perhaps the most concise statement of the Dtr theology of history in the book of Kings is the one given by Gerhard von Rad: for Dtr, history is understood as the accomplishment of Yahweh's words which are proclaimed by his prophets and particularly as the fulfillment of the words of Moses which stand at the beginning of the whole work in Deuteronomy.[99] Yahweh had revealed his commandments to his covenant people; in case of disobedience and infidelity he threatened them with severe judgment; conversely, he promised (material) blessing for those who would act in accordance with his revealed will. These promises and threats were formulated in such a way as to provide a viable interpretation of the great catastrophe of 587—a historical reality which could otherwise have meant nothing less than the final end of the covenant people's *Heilsgeschichte*. Accordingly, the tragic experience was interpreted as the violent actuali-

---

[97] Mowinckel, *Komposition*, p. 36.

[98] Duhm, *Jeremia*, p. xviii.

[99] Gerhard von Rad, *Studies in Deuteronomy* (Chicago: Regnery, 1953), pp. 89ff.

zation of the threats which had come with the promulgation of the Law of Moses and in the prophetic proclamation.

2) The Deuteronomistic tradition, however, did not simply affirm that Yahweh's words were active in Israel's historical experience "as law, judging and destroying but also as gospel, saving and forgiving."[100] The salvific dimension of the word of God in history took shape in the tradition centering on the Davidic dynasty. In the face of Judah's foreseeable extinction, both Dtr and the Jeremianic prose sermons "reflect the hope that Yahweh would be faithful to and fulfill his promises to David"[101] in the unfolding historical experience of the people of God. The "history" of Yahweh with Judah had thus not come to its ultimate end (Dtr: 1 Kgs 2:3, 4; 2 Kgs 17:13ff.; 24:2; 2 Sam 7:12ff.; 2 Kgs 25:27-30; passim; Jer C: 7:12-15, 23-26; 11:3, 6-8; 25:4ff.; 33:14-16, 17ff.; passim). Occasionally the choice between doom and salvation is posed as an alternative for the hearers.

3) The Deuteronomistic theme "according to which Israel's 'turning again' to Yahweh and her obedience to his Law would guarantee her renewed existence as his people"[102] appears in several of the more optimistic passages in the prose tradition (18:7-10, 11b-12; 29:10-14; Dtr: Deut 4:29-31; 1 Kgs 8:46-50).[103]

---

[100]Ibid., p. 89.
[101]Nicholson, *Preaching,* p. 93.
[102]Ibid., p. 81.
[103]Ibid., pp. 87ff.

3

A Redescription of the Correspondences in the Light of Recent Text-Critical Research

RATIONALE AND METHOD

The linguistic, stylistic and theological indices which scholars have employed to assess the relation between the C corpus and Deuteronomistic tradition (in chap. 2) have been described largely on the basis of the MT. The Greek version has been used only to correct the MT where its readings have been deemed significantly problematic or corrupt.[1] E. Würthwein even represents this approach as a basic principle of text criticism when he asserts that "as a general rule M [MT] is to be preferred over all other traditions whenever it cannot be faulted either linguistically or for its material content, unless in particular instances there is good reason for favoring another tradition."[2]

During the last few decades, however, research has yielded good reason to believe that the MT of the book of Jeremiah is only one of two lines of text tradition which can be recovered, and that the other line (surviving in a few Hebrew fragments, and in the ancient Greek version) escaped a significant number of expansions[3] which came to be incorporated in the

---

[1] Even those scholars who generally prefer the LXX of Jeremiah over the MT (e.g., Duhm) still use the traditional text as basis for their exegesis and the LXX only sporadically.

[2] Ernst Würthwein, *The Text of the Old Testament,* trans. Erroll F. Rhodes (Grand Rapids: William B. Eerdmans, 1979), p. 114; so also B. J. Roberts, *The Old Testament Text and Versions* (1951).

[3] The significant divergence in length between the MT and the LXX is of course no new discovery. During the initial years of the critical period, Eichhorn was well aware of the great difference in length between the MT and the LXX and offered his own explanation of the divergence (see his *Einleitung in das Alte Testament,* vol. 4 [Göttingen, 1824], pp. 170-222).

traditional textual witness.[4] Evidence of the second line of text tradition was furnished by fragments from Qumran (4QJer[b])[5] which showed

---

The precise calculation that the MT contains some 2,700 words (plusses) which are absent in the LXX came from the pen of Graf (*Der Prophet Jeremia*[Leipzig: T. O. Weigel, 1862], p. xliii). Until the last few decades, however, the dominant explanation of the divergence in length was that the Greek translator showed a strong tendency to abridge or delete parts of his *Vorlage*. Accordingly, Rudolph could assert "dass 𝔊 nach Kürzung strebt, ist unverkennbar und bei der Breite der Quelle B und C wohl begreiflich" (*Jeremia*, p. xx). In his Harvard dissertation of 1965, John G. Janzen demonstrated that the LXX of the Jeremiah text, far from being defective by haplography, represents rather literally a Hebrew *Vorlage* which is characteristically different from the MT. The MT, he showed, has "undergone much secondary expansion" and thus must be identified as a heavily expanded textual witness (*Studies in the Text of Jeremiah*[Ph.D. dissertation, Harvard University, 1965] = Harvard Semitic Monographs, vol. 6 [Cambridge: Harvard University Press, 1973], pp. 127, 87ff.). For a discussion of Janzen's conclusion see p. 51 below; Young-Jin Min, "The Minuses and Pluses of the LXX Translation of Jeremiah as Compared with the Massoretic Text: Their Classification and Possible Origins" (Ph.D. dissertation, Hebrew University of Jerusalem, 1977), pp. 11ff.; M. Dahood, Review of Janzen in *Biblica* 56 (1975): 429-31.

[4]In a recent paper (February 17, 1981) read at New York University, Emanuel Tov has argued against the rather rigid tripartite characterization of the history of the biblical text (the Palestinian recension, the Egyptian recension, and the Babylonian recension) which is commonly employed, and the accepted terms (such as recension, text-type, text tradition, etc.) which presuppose and often suggest such a framework. In place of these "loaded terms," Tov opts for the utilization of more neutral language (such as source, textual witness, text, etc.) which does not depreciate the great variety of texts, particularly from the finds of Qumran. Although it is too early to assess his argument as a whole, Tov's attempt to clarify our usage of technical language is most welcome. See also S. Talmon, "The Old Testament Text," in *Qumran and the History of the Biblical Text*, ed. F. M. Cross and S. Talmon (Cambridge: Harvard University Press, 1975), pp. 35ff.

[5]4QJer[b], which has been only provisionally published by Janzen (*Studies in the Text of Jeremiah*, pp. 181-84), resembles the LXX (*Vorlage*) in the arrangement of the text and its length. Moreover, Tov has found that 4QJer[b] "shares seven *minuses* with the LXX, of which two are long and five short (mainly names). In addition, there are three minuses in the LXX which are not shared with 4QJer[b], as only a small section of the reconstructed lines of the scroll has been preserved. The reconstructed text of

recently that the Septuagint readings corresponded to actual Hebrew variants and were not, as had been previously suggested, free translations of an Ur-MT.

Frank M. Cross argued in 1965 that 4QJer[b] contains the short textual tradition, "a text type identical with that which underlies the OG translation,"[6] and his student, J. Gerald Janzen, supplied the detailed documentation for the case in his 1965 dissertation. On the basis of the Greek zero-variants (minuses), Janzen substantiated the view that a shorter Hebrew text lies behind the LXX.[7] According to him, the text common to the MT and OG *Vorlage* was handed down to about the mid-fifth or early fourth century B.C.E. before it branched into two independent lines of transmission.[8] This admittedly tentative date for the divergence of the archetypes of the MT and the OG *Vorlage* was based on the observation that the text tradition they have in common already contains corruptions and expansions which would "carry us at least to the mid-fifth century."[9]

While Janzen argued that the two texts represent two different text-traditions (the difference between them being *textual* in nature), Emanuel Tov posited in 1972 and then subsequently that the variation between the MT and OG is the result of intentional *editorial* activity not unlike the Deuteronomistic (editorial) revision of Joshua-Kings. Tov contended that

---

4QJer[b] agrees with the LXX (against MT) in the *sequence* of the verses in ch. 10:1-4, 5a, 9, 5b, 11f. . . ." ("Some Aspects of the Textual and Literary History of the Book of Jeremiah" *Ephemerides Theologicae Lovanienses* 59 (1981) pp. 146f. For a further discussion of 4QJer[b], particularly as it compares to the Greek version, see Young-Jin Min, "Minuses and Pluses."

[6]At the dedication of The Shrine of the Book, April 21, 1965; "The Contribution of the Qumran Discoveries to the Study of the Biblical Text," in *Qumran and the History of the Biblical Text*. "Study of the two textual traditions in the light of the new data makes clear that the Proto-Massoretic text was expansionist, and settles an old controversy . . . . The Septuagint faithfully reflects a conservative Hebrew textual family. On the contrary, Proto-Massoretic and Massoretic family is marked by editorial reworking and conflation, the secondary filling out of names and epithets, expansion from parallel passages, and even glosses from biblical passages outside Jeremiah" (p. 279). See also Nicholson, *Preaching*, pp. 27f., for a similar view.

[7]Janzen, *Studies*. Janzen examined virtually every LXX minus and demonstrated that in most cases the LXX translator could not be accused of abridgement/deleting parts of his text.

[8]Ibid., p. 134.

[9]Ibid.

the OG reflects an earlier edition of Jeremiah (edition I) which differs recensionally from the later text represented by the MT (edition II).[10] Such new reconstructions of the history of the text of Jeremiah make it imperative to reassess the current understandings of the historical development of the prose sermons in the book, and particularly the evidences of its association with Deuteronomic and Deuteronomistic literature and tradition.[11]

This chapter, therefore, examines each of the passages commonly ascribed to this corpus to see how the frequency and distribution of the indices of association in the text common to the Masoretic tradition and the *Vorlage* of the OG compare with their frequency and distribution in the MT. Since the OG *Vorlage* has a shorter text for the book as a whole, we can anticipate that the indices which have been identified in the MT will not always be found in the common text tradition. Some instances will be found instead in the plusses of the MT (i.e., in the text peculiar to the MT). On the whole it is likely that such plusses represent later additions to the text (for the sake of convenience we shall often refer to them as "expansions"), even though it is not possible to be certain about this in every instance because we are not always able to recognize textual corruptions in the OG or its Hebrew *Vorlage*.

To make this comparison, it has been necessary to proceed first by retroversion from the OG translation to its Hebrew *Vorlage*, for it is this *Vorlage* which we shall be comparing to the MT and not the OG translation itself. It should perhaps be noted that such a retroversion leads only

---

[10]"L'Incidence de la critique textuelle sur la critique littéraire dans la livre de Jérémie," *Revue biblique* 79 (1972): 188-99; "Exegetical Notes on the Hebrew Vorlage of the LXX of Jeremiah 27 (34)," *ZAW* 91 (1979): 73-93. According to Tov, the two editions represent two successive Deuteronomistic redactions. The first and more extensive Dtr redaction is reflected in the Hebrew *Vorlage* of the ancient Greek version (= edition I). The second Deuteronomistic layer is to be found in the MT (= edition II).

[11]The need for such an exploration has already been alluded to by Emanuel Tov in his article "L'Incidence"; by Ralph Klein in his monograph *Textual Criticism of the Old Testament* (Philadelphia: Fortress Press, 1974), pp. 34f.; and most recently by Winfried Thiel in *Die deuteronomistische Redaktion von Jeremia 26-45,* p. 122. Thiel says that "die Frage, ob die verschiedenen Textformen der LXX und des M etwa zwei verschiedene (dtr.) Redaktionen repäsentieren" (p. 122) has not been dealt with in his work and needs to be further considered.

to the Hebrew text from which the translator(s) worked, and not to the "original text" which lies ultimately behind it.

The retroversion of the OG Vorlage which underlies the present analysis.—The retroversion offered in this study is to a large extent modeled—in principle but not always in format—upon Emanuel Tov's pilot study "Exegetical Notes on the Hebrew *Vorlage* of the LXX of Jeremiah 27 (34)." Moreover, it complies with the guidelines set forth cogently by Tov in his book *The Text-Critical Use of the Septuagint in Biblical Research.*[12] Ziegler's resultant text, which is at present the most responsible critical edition of the OG, serves as textual base for our retroversion of the C material.[13]

Retroversion from the OG translation of Jeremiah is made easier by its relatively literal character.[14] This is especially true of the translation of the prose sections which are at times almost woodenly literal.[15] It is also a help that in the C corpus the majority of its variant readings involve differences which are quantitative (i.e., plusses and minuses) rather than

---

[12]Emanuel Tov, *The Text-Critical Use of the Septuagint in Biblical Research* (Jerusalem: Simor Press, 1982).

[13]The tools employed in this retroversion include: Joseph Ziegler, *Septuaginta. Ieremias, Baruch, Threni Epistula Ieremiae,* Vetus Testamentum Graecum, Auctoritate Societatis Litterarum Gottingensis Editum, vol. 15 (Göttingen: Vandenhoeck & Ruprecht, 1957); W. Rudolph, *Liber Jeremiae,* Biblia Hebraica Stuttgartensia 8 (Stuttgart: Württembergische Bibelanstalt, 1970); E. Hatch and H. Redpath, *A Concordance to the Septuagint and the Other Greek Versions of the Old Testament* (Oxford: Clarendon, 1897); E. Camilo dos Santos, *An Expanded Hebrew Index for the Hatch-Redpath Concordance to the Septuagint* (Jerusalem: Dugith [1973]); Solomon Mandelkern, *Veteris Testamenti Concordantiae Hebraicae atque Chaldaicae,* 9th ed. (Jerusalem: Schocken, 1971).

[14]Movers, Scholz, Tov, and Min have argued convincingly that in the vast majority of cases the Greek translation of its *Vorlage* was relatively literal; see F. C. Movers, *De utriusque recensionis vaticiniorum Ieremiae, graecae alexandrinae et hebraicae masorethicae, indole et origine commentatio critica* (Hamburg: Perthes, 1837), pp. 7-9; A. Scholz, *Der masorethische Text und die LXX-Uebersetzung des Buches Jeremias* (Regensburg: Manz, 1875), pp. 22-28; Tov, "Exegetical," pp. 74f.; Min, "Minuses and Pluses," pp. 183ff. This is now also substantiated by the analysis of Bernard M. Zlotowitz, *The Septuagint Translation of the Hebrew Terms in Relation to God in the Book of Jeremiah* (New York: Ktav, 1981).

[15]Tov, "Exegetical," p. 75.

qualitative (i.e., content variants and transpositions).[16] In interpreting the OG minuses we have followed the working hypothesis that they represent minuses in the Hebrew *Vorlage,* a working hypothesis which we believe Janzen and Tov have amply justified for Jeremiah.[17] A problem arises only in those few instances where haplography may be suspected, since it is virtually impossible to discern whether such lapses were already present in the *Vorlage* or were made during the process of textual transmission. For our purposes the problem is finally irrelevant, however, since retroversion is not an end in itself, but only a step toward distinguishing those readings which are peculiar to the MT from those which are common to both lines of text transmission. At that point we shall have to reckon any reading which has been omitted from either line through scribal error as common text, no matter when the lapse took place.

Qualitative differences are more difficult to assess, especially when they are minor. The problem of discovering variants in such cases has been discussed by Tov, who notes that

> like all translators, the translators of the LXX changed several details of their *Vorlage* in accordance with the con-textual requirements, the need of the target language, and their literary taste. Among these changes, often very small, one finds several harmonizing changes of incongruities, such as disharmony in the use of pronouns, nouns, verbal forms, as well as number . . . . Thus, as a rule, it cannot be known whether a particular change of the mentioned type was made by the translator himself or was already present in his *Vorlage,* because we lack the necesssary knowledge in order to distinguish between the two levels.[18]

To be sure, variants of this sort are less important for our purposes than plusses and minuses. They are nevertheless a reminder that no retroversion can claim to provide an exact replica of the text which lay before the translator.

The format employed for representing the text.—In the discussion which follows, the Hebrew text of each passage is supplied. We have represented the results of our comparison of the MT and the *Vorlage* of

---

[16]Ibid., pp. 77f.
[17]See Janzen, *Studies;* Tov, "Exegetical," pp. 74ff.
[18]Tov, "Exegetical," pp. 78f., n. 25.

the OG by printing all the readings which are common to these witnesses (= C') in large type, and all the readings which are peculiar to the MT (= C+) in small type. Where there are minor content differences of the sort discussed above (i.e., differences in number, person, verbal form, etc.), we have simply printed the MT and placed a supralinear X after the word. More important content variants, and the few Greek plusses, are often mentioned in footnotes. The orthography follows that of the MT as does the numbering of chapters and verses.

The outline followed in the discussion of each passage.—Each of the passages commonly ascribed to the C corpus will be discussed in turn, following this basic outline:

a. A summary statement calling attention to the most significant differences between the MT and the OG *Vorlage*.

b. The text of the passage, in the format described above. To aid the analysis which follows, the linguistic indices which we have catalogued in the preceding chapter will be underlined. A solid underlining indicates that the word or phrase appears in the passage just as we have listed it in the catalog; a broken underlining indicates some difference in wording.

c. A list of all the linguistic indices which have been identified in the passage, in the order in which they appear in our catalog. This tabulation includes the following data:

   i.   The type of diction employed (see our catalog for the four categories of diction).

   ii. Our catalog number for the particular word or phrase.

   iii. The verse in which the word or phrase occurs (in parentheses).

   iv. The presence or absence of the word or phrase in C' and C, marked in parallel columns by the use of the following sigla:

   -    to mark the absence of the word or phrase

   X   to mark the presence of the word or phrase

   X*   to indicate that the word or phrase in the text differs in some respect from the diction we have indexed

   Xc   to indicate that subsequent expansion (C+) has filled out a word or phrase in C' to complete—or actually to create—the indexed expression.

d. A summary tabulation of the instances of indexed language by type of diction.

e. Commentary, which reviews the other evidences of association with Deuteronomistic tradition which have been seen in the passage, and assesses the extent to which these are the result of subsequent expansion.

THE PASSAGES COMMONLY ASCRIBED
TO THE C CORPUS

3:6-13

This passage has been transmitted in the two text traditions with relatively few qualitative variants. The MT has a few plusses, but these phrases do not introduce significant changes. Tov is probably right that κατοικια (vv. 6, 8, 12) "should be considered as an etymological translation of משב(ו)בה on the basis of ישב."[19]

(6) ויאמר יהוה אלי בימי יאשיהו המלך הראית אשר
עשתה^x משבה^x ישראל הלכה^x היא^x על–כל–הר גבה ואל–
תחת כל–עץ רענן ותזני^{–x}–שם: (7) ואמר אחרי עשותה
את–כל–אלה אלי תשוב ולא–שבה ותראה בגודה^x אחותה
יהודה: (8) וארא כי על–כל–אדות אשר נאפה משבה^x
ישראל שלחתיה^x ואתן את–ספר כריתתיה^x אליה ולא
יראה בגדה יהודה אחותה ותלך ותזן גם–היא: (9) והיה
מקל זנותה ותחנף את–הארץ ותנאף ^xאת–האבן ואת–העץ^x:
(10) וגם^{–x}–בכל–זאת לא–שבה אלי בגודה אחותה יהודה
בכל–לבה כי אם–בשקר נאם יהוה: (11) ויאמר יהוה אלי
צדקה נפשה משבה ישראל מבגדה יהודה: (12) הלך וקראת את–
הדברים האלה צפונה ואמרת שובה^x משבה^x ישראל נאם–
יהוה לוא^x–אפיל פני בכם כי–חסיד אני נאם–יהוה לא^x
אטור^x לעולם: (13) אך דעי עונך כי ביהוה אלהיך
פשעת ותפזרי את–דרכיך לזרים תחת כל–עץ רענן
<u>ובקולי לא–שמעתם נאם–יהוה</u>:

---

[19]Emanuel Tov, *The Septuagint Translation of Jeremiah and Baruch* (Missoula, Montana: Scholars Press, 1976), p. 138.

		C'	C		C'	C
Type I:	1. (vs. 13)	X	X	23. (vs. 6)	X	X
	17. (vs. 10)	X	X	28. (vs. 10)	X	X

Summary Tabulation of Instances

	I	II	III	IV	total
C':	4	-	-	-	4
C+	-	-	-	-	-
C:	4	-	-	-	4

Both Duhm and Mowinckel considered 3:6-13 a secondary accretion from the hand of a supplementor (Duhm) or a Deuteronomistic editor (Mowinckel).[20] Mowinckel included it in his late Deuteronomistic C source with other passages which lack the characteristic introductory sentence. He noted that this passage, which he referred to as an entreaty to Israel or Ephraim, disturbs the continuity between vv. 1-5 and 19f. (A). Verses 6-13, he argued, form a late Deuteronomistic parallel to the authentic Jeremianic oracle in vv. 1-5, 19f. and were probably inserted in their present place owing to their similar theme. Although both oracles take the form of an accusation against unfaithful Judah and assert similarly that a return to Yahweh is no longer possible for Judah (because of her many sins), the original saying never mentions Ephraim at all. While Mowinckel did not discuss the provenience of vv. 6-13, Thiel has argued for an exilic and specifically Deuteronomistic provenience on the basis of the passage's didactic style and its emphasis on the sin of idolatry, as Judah's gravest and most profound act of infidelity.[21] Furthermore, the condemnation of worship on the "high places"—a strictly forbidden cultic practice for the Deuteronomistic school—suggests strongly an exilic Dtr hand. Hyatt has observed, moreover, that vs. 8, with its reference to faithless Israel's decree of divorce (on account of her uninhibited harlotry) and its usage of technical terminology, "to send away, to divorce," and "bill of divorce," is reminiscent of the Deuteronomic law of divorce (Deut

---

[20]Duhm, *Das Buch Jeremia*, pp. 35ff.; Mowinckel, *Komposition*, pp. 42f.

[21]Thiel, *Die deuteronomistische Redaktion*, 1-25, p. 89.

24:1).[22] Bright, however, has found the diction and motifs of this passage to be entirely congruent with Jeremianic poetry and the earlier prophecies of Hosea. Although he ascribes the passage to the reign of Josiah, Bright concedes that the prose monologue probably received its present form later, perhaps after 587. According to him, vv. 6-13 serve to "apply the hope which Jeremiah had once extended to northern Israel to the situation of the exiles in Babylon."[23]

As the above analysis shows, the characteristic C features are fully represented in C'; the summary tabulation indicates that all four instances of Type I diction are attested in C'. The variants which C+ has introduced into C' are not linguistic or theological indices of the C corpus, but rather words and phrases attested outside the Deuteronomic, Deuteronomistic, or Jeremianic prose tradition (e.g., ארץ + חנף Num 35:33, Ps 106:38).

7:1-8:3

A basic discrepancy between the lines of text tradition concerns the locale in which the oracle (vv. 1-15) was delivered. In both, the oracle deals with the misuse of the cult of the Jerusalem temple, but the OG *Vorlage* does not seem to indicate that the prophet uttered his oracle there. It lacks the clauses in vv. 1f. and the demonstrative adjective in vv. 10 and 11 which refer explicitly to a temple locale. The only doubt is whether it understood the references to "this place" (במקום הזה) in vv. 3, 6, and 7 where במקום הזה stands in apposition to (בארץ) to refer to the "land" or to the "temple." The MT clearly assumes a temple location as the superscription (vv. 1-2) and the demonstrative adjectives ("this house" passim) show. It appears that the explicit reference to the temple locale was added to C' after the divergence of the two lines of text transmission, probably on the basis of chap. 26.

(1) הדבר אשר היה אל־ירמיהו מאת יהוה לאמר: (2) עמד
בשער בית יהוה וקראת צם את־הדבר הזה ואמרת שמעו דבר־
יהוה כל־יהודה הבאים בשערים האלה להשתחות ליהוה:
(3) כה־אמר יהוה צבאות אלהי ישראל היטיבו דרכיכם ומעלליכם
ואשכנה אתכם במקום הזה: (4) אל־תבטחו לכם אל־דברי השקר[1]

---

[22]Hyatt, "Jeremiah and Deuteronomy," p. 171.
[23]J. Bright, *Jeremiah*, p. 27.

[1]OG adds *hoti to parapon ouk ōphelēsousin humas.*

לאמר היכל יהוה היכל יהוה היכל יהוה המה^x: (5) כי^xאם־
היטיב תיטיבו את־דרכיכם ואת־מעלליכם אם־עשו תעשו משפט
בין איש ובין רעהו: (6) גר^x יתום^x ואלמנה לא תעשקו ודם
נקי אל־תשפכו במקום הזה ואחרי אלהים אחרים לא תלכו לרע לכם:
(7) ושכנתי אתכם במקום הזה בארץ אשר נתתי לאבותיכם למן־
עולם ועד־עולם: (8) הנה אתם בטחים^x לכם^x על־דברי השקר
לבלתי הועיל: (9) הגנב^x רצח ונאף והשבע לשקר וקטר לבעל
והלך אחרי אלהים אחרים אשר לא־ידעתם³: (10) ובאתם ועמדתם
לפני בבית הזה אשר נקרא־שמי עליו ואמרתם נצלנו למען עשות
את כל־התועבות האלה: (11) המערת פרצים היה^x הבית הזה⁴
אשר־נקרא־שמי עליו בעיניכם גם אנכי הנה ראיתי נאם־יהוה:
(12) כי לכו־נא^x אל־מקומי אשר בשילו אשר שכנתי שמי שם
בראשונה וראו את אשר־עשיתי לו מפני רעת עמי ישראל: (13)
ועתה יען עשותכם את־כל־המעשים האלה נאם יהוה ואדבר
אליכם השכם השכם ודבר ולא שמעתם^x ואקרא אתכם ולא עניתם: (14)
ועשיתי לבית אשר נקרא־שמי עליו אשר אתם בטחים בו ולמקום
אשר־נתתי לכם ולאבותיכם כאשר עשיתי לשלו: (15) והשלכתי
אתכם מעל פני כאשר השלכתי את־כל־אחיכם את כל־זרע אפרים:
(16) ואתה אל־תתפלל בעד־העם הזה ואל־תשא ⁵בעדם רנה⁵
ותפלה^x ואל־תפגע־בי^x כי־אינני שמע אתך^x: (17) האינך ראה מה
המה עשים בערי יהודה ובחצות ירושלם: (18) הבנים^x מלקטים
עצים והאבות מבערים את־האש והנשים^x לשות בצק לעשות
כונים למלכת^x השמים והסך נסכים לאלהים אחרים למען הכעסני:
(19) האתי הם מכעסים נאם־יהוה הלוא אתם למען בשת פניהם:
(20) לכן כה־אמר אדני יהוה הנה אפי וחמתי נתכם אל^x־
המקום הזה על^x־האדם ועל־הבהמה ועל^x־עץ השדה ועל־פרי
האדמה ובערה ולא תכבה: (21) כה אמר יהוה צבאות אלהי
ישראל עלותיכם ספו על־זבחיכם ואכלו בשר: (22) כי לא־
דברתי את־אבותיכם ולא צויתים ביום הוציאי אותם מארץ
מצרים על־דברי^x עולה וזבח: (23) כי אם־את־הדבר הזה צויתי
אותם לאמר שמעו בקולי והייתי לכם לאלהים ואתם תהיו־לי
לעם והלכתם בכל־הדרך^x אשר אצוה אתכם למען ייטב לכם: (24)
ולא שמעו^x ולא־הטו את־אזנם וילכו במעצות⁷ בשררות לבם הרע

---

²OG may be defective by haplography.
³OG adds *tou kakōs einai humin.*
⁴OG reads *ho oikos mou.*
⁵OG transposes.
⁶OG reads *stratia.*
⁷May be absent in OG by haplography.

ויהיו לאחור ולא לפנים: (25) למׄן-היום אשרˣ יצאו
אבותיכםˣ מארץ מצרים עד היום הזה ואשלח אליכם את-כל-
עבדי הנביאים יום השכם ושלחˣ: (26) ולוא שמעו אלי
ולא הטו את-אזנם ויקשו את-ערפם הרעו מאבותם: (27)
ודברת אליהם את-כל-הדבריםˣ האלהˣ ולא ישמעו אליך
וקראת אליהם ולא יענוכה: (28) ואמרת אליהם זה הגוי
אשר לוא-שמעו בקול יהוה אלהיו ולא לקחו מוסר אבדה
האמונה ונכרתה מפיהם: (29) גזי נזרך והשליכי ושאי
על-שפיםˣ קינה כי מאס יהוה ויטש את-דור עברתוˣ:
(30) כי-עשו בני-יהודה הרע בעיני נאם-יהוה שמו
שקוציהם בבית אשר נקרא-שמי עליו לטמאו: (31) ובנו
במותˣ התפת אשר בגיא בן-הנם לשרף את-בניהם ואת-
בנתיהם באש אשר לא צויתיˣ ולא עלתה על-לבי: (32)
לכן הנה-ימים באים נאם-יהוה ולא-יאמר עוד[8] התפת
וגיא בן-הנם כי אם-גיא ההרנה וקברו בתפת מאין מקום:
(33) והיתה נבלת העם הזה למאכל לעוף השמים ולבהמת
הארץ ואין מחריד: (34) והשבתי מערי יהודה ומחצות
ירושלם קול ששון וקול שמחה קול חתן וקול כלה כי
לחרבה תהיהˣ הארץ: (8:1) בעת ההיא נאם-יהוה ויציאוˣ
את-עצמות מלכי-יהודה ואת-עצמותˣ-שריו ואת-עצמות
הכהנים ואת עצמות הנביאים ואת עצמות יושבי-
ירושלם מקבריהם: (2) ושטחום לשמש ולירח[9] ולכל
צבא השמים אשר אהבוםˣ ואשר עבדוםˣ ואשר הלכו
אחריהם ואשר דרשוםˣ ואשר השתחוו להם לא יאספו
ולא יקברו לדמן[10] על-פני האדמה יהיוˣ: (3) ונבחרˣ
מות מחיים לכל השארית הנשארים מן-המשפחה הרעה
הזאתˣ בכל-המקמותˣ הנשארים אשר הדחתים שם נאם
יהוה צבאות:

---

[8] OG adds *bōmos*.

[9] OG adds *kai pros pantas tous asteras*, which, however, Ziegler brackets; cf. Deut 4:19.

[10] OG reads *paradeigma*.

		C'	C		C'	C
Type I:	1. (vs. 23)	X	X	5. (vs. 25)	X	X
	1. (vs. 28)	X	X	7. (vs. 18)	X	X
	2. (vs. 22)	X	X	9. (vs. 30)	X	X
	2. (vs. 25)	X	X	13. (vs. 6)	X	X
	3. (vs. 6)	X	X	19. (vs. 30)	X	X
	3. (vs. 9)	X	X	21. (vs. 23)	X	X
	4. (vs. 7)	X	X	29. (vs. 23)	X	X
	4. (vs. 14)	X	X	30. (vs. 25)	X	X
				33. (vs. 15)	X	X
Type II:	38. (vs. 9)	X	X	43. (vs. 32)	X	X
	40. (vs. 10)	X	X	44. (vs. 23)	X	X
	40. (vs. 11)	X	X	46. (vs. 26)	X	X
	40. (vs. 14)	X	X	47. (8:2)	X	X
	40. (vs. 30)	X	X	48. (vs. 16)	X	X
Type III:	52. (8:3)	X	X	55. (vs. 9)	X	X
	53. (vs. 33)	X	X	58. (vs. 6)	X	X
	54. (vs. 24)	X	X	67. (vs. 12)	X	X
Type IV:	68. (vs. 3)	-	Xc	79. (vs. 28)	X	X
	68. (vs. 21)	-	Xc	82. (vs. 3)	X	X
	70. (vs. 13)	-	X	82. (vs. 5)	X	X
	70. (vs. 25)	X	X	83. (vs. 2)	-	X
	71. (vs. 1)	-	X	84. (vs. 31)	X	X
	72. (vs. 24)	X	X	85. (8:2)	X	X
	72. (vs. 26)	X	X	87. (vs. 4)	X	X
	73. (vs. 20)	X	X	87. (vs. 8)	X	X
	74. (vs. 17)	X	X	88. (8:1)	X	X
	74. (vs. 34)	X	X	89. (vs. 13)	X	X
	78. (vs. 34)	X	X	89. (vs. 27)	-	X

Summary Tabulation of Instances

	I	II	III	IV	totals
C':	17	10	6	16	49
C+:	-	-	-	6	6
C:	17	10	6	22	55

The overwhelming majority of scholars have recognized that 7:1-8:3 is filled with Deuteronomistic diction and is written in a typically Deuteronomic style.[24] The analysis of the linguistic indices given above confirms this judgment. Much of the text is indexed diction, and almost half (49%) of this diction is Type I or Type II (i.e., diction attested at least once in the Deuteronomistic corpus). With respect to style, the passage has been characterized as verbose, rhetorical, and as having the Dtr *Alternativ-Predigt* (the introductory formula [vs.1], the prophetic commission to go and speak [vs. 2ab], the command to hear the prophetic proclamation [vs. 2c], the messenger formula [vs. 3a], the introductory imperative [vv. 3b, 4a], alternative I [vv. 5b, 6ab], the promise of salvation [vs. 7], alternative II [vv. 8, 13], announcement of judgment [vv. 14, 15]).[25]

Those who generally regard the prose sermons as expansion or recasting the Jeremianic tradition in a subsequent period have come to agree with their critics that many of the ideas expressed in this long section do not run counter to the general direction of the poetic oracles in the book. Accordingly, these scholars have argued, for example, that the passage preserves the "substance" (Hyatt), "spirit" (Rudolph), or *"Tendenz"* (Thiel) of genuine oracles of the prophet. In particular, the condemnation of the people's superficial confidence in the Jerusalem temple, the general attitude toward the cultus and sacrifice (e.g., vv. 21ff.), and the moral basis of the prophetic appeal all conform to ideas and motifs which find expression in the undisputed oracular addresses of Jeremiah. The passage's theology of history corresponds to Deuteronomistic theology and, depending upon one's understanding of the redaction history of Jeremiah, is

---

[24]See especially Mowinckel, *Komposition*, p. 31; Hyatt, "Deuteronomic Edition," p. 80; *The Book of Jeremiah*, pp. 867-79; Rudolph, *Jeremia*, pp. 44ff.; Bright, *Jeremiah*, pp. 58f.; cf., however, Weippert, *Prosareden*, pp. 41ff.

[25]Thiel, *Die deuteronomistische Redaktion*, 1-25, pp. 290ff.

viewed either as a later recasting of the Jeremianic tradition or as integral to the prophetic tradition from its outset. The destruction of Judah
and the Jerusalem temple is the judgment of Yahweh upon his people's
sins, and specifically their illegitimate worship. Shiloh's fate, appealed to
as a foreboding historical precedent, is also traced to Israel's "wickedness"
(vs. 12b). The underlying concern, according to Thiel and others, is to give
an acceptable explanation of the impending event of 587 from a Deuteronomistic perspective. Accordingly, the passage asserts that the covenant
people have brought (or are in the process of bringing) the disaster upon
themselves; Yahweh is thus exempt from all wrongdoing, since he has only
acted in accordance with the covenant stipulation.

Most of the variations between C' and C have no direct bearing on the
question at hand. In the majority of cases, C supplies fuller epithets for
divinity (of which several are pertinent to the present inquiry), additional
prophetic formulae, supplementary information concerning location, and
various other minor plusses. While the majority of the characteristic C
features are already present in C', several have been introduced by C+.
Six of the fifty-five instances of indexed diction have been added to C' by
C+; all are Type IV (i.e., unattested in Deuteronomy or in Dtr). C' lacks
the introductory formula which Mowinckel and others have regarded as
the main indicator of the C corpus. Two of the initial parts of the *Alternativ-Predigt* (the introductory formula in vs. 1 and the prophetic commission to go and speak in vs. 2) are lacking in C'. Accordingly, the *Stilform* is actually attested only in the expanded text, and not in the earlier
common text tradition. C' relates the theme of the covenant people's
continuing rebellion and disobedience, but C accentuates this and develops
it further: to the charge that the fathers did not listen to the prophets
because they were bent on evil (vv. 25f.) C adds that Jeremiah will not be
heeded either (vs. 27). In general the C features are distributed fairly
evenly throughout the text of C', although they are grouped most densely
in vv. 1-6, 22-26, 33f.

11:1-14

With the exception of two quantitative variants of some consequence,
the MT and OG *Vorlage* are in remarkable agreement. There are few
incongruities of any type; that is to say, the witnesses agree for the most
part in their verbal forms, sentence structure, and general arrangement.
Moreover, the translator employed Greek-Hebrew equivalents which have
a very high frequency, so retroversion is relatively easy. The two significant variants occur in vv. 13, 7f. Janzen has explained the MT plus in

vs. 13 as a probable conflation of מזבחות לקטר לבעל and מזבחות לבשת,
which was created "by the otherwise well-known replacement of בעל by
בשת."[26] The lengthy variant in vv. 7f. (15 percent or 36 of the 239 words
of the MT)[27] is far more important to the present study. Scholars disagree
whether the OG here is defective by haplography (Cornill and Skinner), a
deliberate abridgement (Rudolph), or indeed reflects an earlier stage of
the text tradition (Janzen and others). Cornill's reason for viewing the OG
as defective by haplography is based on the observation that ולא עשו/και
ουκ εποιησαν (vs. 8) "lacks a proper subject and comes too abruptly after
verse 6 for ₲ [i.e., the OG translation] to be original."[28] Owing to the
repetition of some phrases and the similar content of vv. 3ff. and vv. 7f.,
Rudolph argues that the OG translator probably deleted vv. 7f. deliber-
ately. Janzen objects to Rudolph's argument on the grounds that the
passages in question are in no way identical. "One relates the single
historical covenant event vv. 3ff , while the other elaborates the familiar
theme of Israel's continuing rebellion and disobedience in the face of
Yahweh's constant exhortation to covenant loyalty [vv. 7f.]."[29] With
respect to the difficult reading ולא עשו , he suggests that it may have
served originally as a transitional gloss from vs. 6 to vs. 9. Verses 7-8 are
thus most likely secondary, drawn from Deuteronomistic language elsewhere in the book.

(1) הדבר אשר היה אל־ירמיהו מאת יהוה לאמר: (2)
שמעו את־דברי הברית הזאת ודברתם[X] אל־איש יהודה
ועל[X]־ישבי ירושלם: (3) ואמרת אליהם כה־אמר יהוה
אלהי ישראל ארור האיש אשר לא ישמע את־דברי
הברית הזאת: (4) אשר צויתי את־אבותיכם ביום
הוציאי־אותם מארץ־מצרים מכור הברזל לאמר שמעו
בקולי ועשיתם אותם ככל אשר־אצוה אתכם והייתם לי
לעם ואנכי אהיה לכם לאלהים: (5) למען הקים את־
השבועה[X] אשר־נשבעתי לאבותיכם לתת להם ארץ זבת
חלב ודבש כיום הזה ואען ואמר אמן יהוה: (6)
ויאמר יהוה אלי קרא את־כל־הדברים האלה בערי
יהודה ובחצות ירושלם לאמר שמעו את־דברי הברית
הזאת ועשיתם אותם: (7) כי העד העדתי באבותיכם ביום

---

[26]Janzen, *Studies*, p. 12.
[27]For an explanation of our word count, see p. 119 below.
[28]Janzen, *Studies*, p. 39.
[29]Ibid.

העלותי אותם מארץ מצרים ועד-היום הזה השכם והעד
לאמר שמעו בקולי: (8) ולא שמעו ולא-הטו את-אזנם
וילכו איש בשרירות לבם הרע ואביא עליהם את-כל-
דברי הברית-הזאת אשר-צויתי לעשות ולא עשו: (9)
ויאמר יהוה אלי נמצא-קשר באיש יהודה ובישבי
ירושלם: (10) שבו על-עונת אבותם הראשנים אשר מאנו
לשמוע את-דברי והמה^{x} הלכו אחרי אלהים אחרים לעבדם
הפרו בית-ישראל ובית יהודה את-בריתי אשר כרתי את-
אבותם: (11) לכן כה אמר יהוה הנני מביא אליהם^{1} רעה^{x}
אשר^{x} לא-יוכלו לצאת ממנה וזעקו אלי ולא אשמע אליהם:
(12) והלכו ערי יהודה וישבי ירושלם וזעקו אל-
האלהים אשר הם מקטרים להם והושע לא-יושיעו להם
בעת רעתם: (13) כי מספר עריך היו אלהיך יהודה
ומספר חצות ירושלם שמתם מזבחות לבשת מזבחות לקטר
לבעל: (14) ואתה אל-תתפלל בעד-העם הזה ואל-תשא
בעדם רנה ותפלה כי אינני שמע בעת קראם אלי בעד^{x}
רעתם:

		C'	C			C'	C
Type I:	1. (vs. 4)	X	X	10. (vs. 11)		X	X
	1. (vs. 7)	–	X	14. (vs. 5)		X	X
	2. (vs. 4)	X	X	16. (vs. 5)		X	X
	2. (vs. 7)	–	X	24. (vs. 4)		X	X
	3. (vs. 10)	X	X				
Type II:	38. (vs. 12)	X	X	42. (vs. 3)		X	X
	38. (vs. 13)	X	X	42. (vs. 6)		X	X
	41. (vs. 2)	X	X	42. (vs. 8)		–	X
	41. (vs. 9)	X	X	44. (vs. 4)		X	X
	42. (vs. 2)	X	X	48. (vs. 14)		X	X
Type III:	54. (vs. 8)	–	X	66. (vs. 5)		X	X
	65. (vs. 3)	X	X				
Type IV:	70. (vs. 7)	–	X	72. (vs. 8)		–	X
	71. (vs. 1)	X	X	74. (vs. 6)		X	X

---

[1]OG reads *epi ton laon touton kaka.*

Summary Tabulation of Instances

	I	II	III	IV	totals
C':	7	9	2	2	20
C+:	2	1	1	2	6
C:	9	10	3	4	26

The number of characteristic C features in this passage is proportionately larger than any other in the book. As is immediately apparent from the above collation, linguistic indices are dispersed relatively evenly throughout the passage, although most densely grouped in vv. 7f. An unusually high proportion (73 percent) of these indices is attested at least once in Dtr. Several long phrases of Deuteronomy occur in this passage almost verbatim (vs. 3 = Deut 27:26; vs. 4 = Deut 4:20; vs. 5 = Deut 7:8, 8:18, 9:5, 27:15; vs. 8 = Deut 4:13; vv. 2, 3, 6, 8 in part = Deut 28:29).[30]

There has been much controversy about the interpretation of the passage in its present form. The majority have argued that 11:1-14 was originally intended "to show that Jeremiah supported Deuteronomy and even became an itinerant evangelist for the reforms of Josiah."[31] For Duhm, an early representative of this point of view, the passage depicts Yahweh summoning Judah to obey the terms of the covenant through his wandering emissary (*Reiseprediger*) for the Deuteronomic law (namely, Jeremiah), and subsequently revealing to the prophet his decree to destroy the covenant people on account of their incessant disobedience. In his view, the passage is thoroughly fictitious and hagadic.[32] Rudolph argues that there is no good reason to doubt that an authentic tradition lies behind this C passage, however, since it corresponds throughout with the views of the poetic Jeremiah. He contends that Duhm and others have too easily dismissed this as legendary, i.e., as a report which makes the prophet into a supporter of Deuteronomy and an evangelist for the Deuteronomic reform of 621. Rudolph understands the covenant referred to in 11:1ff. to be the Sinai covenant and not the Deuteronomic (or Moab) covenant. Accordingly, the prophet is portrayed as one who stands up for the Sinai covenant "whose binding worth he recognizes anew for himself"

---

[30]See Rudolph, *Jeremia*, p. 67; Hyatt, "Deuteronomic Edition," p. 80.

[31]Hyatt, "Jeremiah and Deuteronomy," p. 168.

[32]Duhm, *Jeremia*, pp. 106ff.

(vv. 3-5).[33] We have here, he suggests, the familiar reproach of a prophetic oracle, that the present people of God are no better than the
ancestors. Jeremiah declares that the disobedience of the people towards
Yahweh is a formal renunciation, a rebellion (vs. 9), for they have not
fulfilled their covenant obligations. Therefore, Yahweh allows the pun-
ishments of the covenant for disobedience to come upon them.

The texts of C' and C have no substantial differences, except for
vv. 7f. and vs. 13. The variant in vs. 13 has no bearing on the question at
hand. This is not true of the variant in vv. 7f. First, these verses are
crammed with characteristic C diction—the density of these indices is
proportionately greater than in any other two consecutive verses in the C
corpus. Furthermore, it is only in these verses that the motif of Israel's
incessant and obdurate rebellion and disobedience—an index of C's theology according to Mowinckel and others—is expressed. Finally, vs. 8 is one
of the few passages in the C material (or in any stratum of the book)
which refers to Yahweh's judgment upon his people (i.e., the *Unheil* of
587) as a *past* historical reality. Other passages allude to the destruction
of Jerusalem and the subsequent exile to Babylon as still imminent events.
This has been thought to provide a *terminus a quo* for the passage as a
whole. Since these verses are evidently a C+ expansion, the argument is
irrelevant for the earlier literary stage of the text.

16:1-15

In addition to the relatively minor differences between the MT and the
Vorlage of the OG, three of which have been identified by Janzen as MT
expansions from parallel or related contexts,[34] the textual witnesses
diverge at three significant points. First, the introductory sentence is
unattested in the OG *Vorlage* (vs. 1),[35] yet without the introductory

---

[33]Rudolph, *Jeremia*, p. 68.

[34]Janzen, *Studies*, p. 40.

[35]Accordingly, Janzen argues that the OG "preserves a text which
stood one stage closer than 𝕸 to a poetic form, in which Jeremiah was
instructed not to marry. The original poetic form was elaborated to its
present prose form" (*Studies,* p. 113). Janzen makes here both a text-
critical and literary-critical judgment. His text-critical claim that the OG
preserves a more original tradition is well supported. His assumption that
the original tradition was a poetic/oracle form, although possible, has not
been established. Such an assumption does not allow for the possibility
that the material may never have been part of the authentic Jeremianic
tradition but may have originated later in its present prose form.

formula the text still reflects the autobiographical style which is typical
of several C passages. Second, the MT and OG *Vorlage* differ in their
images of the imminent destruction coming upon the Palestinian inhabitants (vs. 4). Lastly, the MT adds a long sentence in vv. 5b-6a which
apparently serves to intensify the destruction of desolation in the land and
to heighten the seriousness of Yahweh's displeasure by employing additional images of destruction (*Unheil*).

(1) ויהי דבר-יהוה אלי לאמר: (2) לא-תקח לך^X אשה ^{1}
ולא-יהיו לך בנים ובנות במקום הזה: (3) כי-כה אמר
יהוה על-הבנים ועל-הבנות הילודים במקום הזה ועל-
אמתם הילדות אותם ועל-אבותם המולדים אותם בארץ
הזאת: (4) ממותי^X תחלאים ימתו לא יספדו ולא יקברו
לדמן^2 על-פני האדמה יהיו ^{3}ובחרב וברעב יכלו והיתה
נבלתם למאכל לעוף השמים ולבהמת הארץ^3: (5) כי-כה
אמר יהוה אל-תבוא בית מרזח ואל-תלך לספוד ואל-תנד
להם כי-אספתי את-שלומי מאת העם-הזה נאם-יהוה את-
החסד ואת-הרחמים: (6) ומתו גדלים וקטנים בארץ הזאת
לא יקברו ולא-יספדו להם ולא יתגדד^X ולא יקרח להם^X:
(7) ולא-יפרסו^X להם^X על^X-אבל^X לנחמו על-מת ולא^X-
ישקו אותם^X כוס תנחומים על-אביו ועל-אמו: (8) ובית^X-
משתה לא-תבוא לשבת אותם^X לאכל ולשתות: (9) כי כה
אמר יהוה צבאות אלהי ישראל הנני משבית מן-המקום
הזה לעיניכם ובימיכם קול ששון וקול שמחה קול חתן
וקול כלה: (10) והיה כי תגיד לעם הזה את כל-הדברים
האלה ואמרו אליך על-מה דבר יהוה עלינו את כל-הרעה^X
הגדולה הזאת^X ומה עוננו ומה חטאתנו אשר חטאנו ליהוה
אלהינו: (11) ואמרת אליהם על אשר-עזבו^X אבותיכם
אותי נאם-יהוה וילכו אחרי אלהים אחרים ויעבדום
וישתחוו להם ואתי עזבו ואת-תורתי לא שמרו: (12) ואתם
הרעתם לעשות מאבותיכם והנכם הלכים איש אחרי שררות
לבו^X-הרע לבלתי שמע אלי: (13) והטלתי אתכם מעל הארץ
הזאת על^X-הארץ אשר לא ידעתם אתם ואבותיכם ועבדתם-
שם את-אלהים אחרים יומם ולילה אשר לא-אתן^X לכם חנינה:
(14) לכן הנה-ימים באים נאם-יהוה ולא-יאמר^X עוד חי-

---

^{1}OG adds *legei kurios ho theos Israēl.*

^{2}OG reads *paradeigma.*

^{3}OG reads *tois thrēiois tēs gēs kai tois peteinois tou ouranou en
machaira pesountai kai en limō suntelesthēsontai.*

יהוה אשר העלה את־בני ישראל מארץ מצרים: (15) כי אם־
חי־יהוה אשר העלה את־בני^X ישראל מארץ צפון ומכל
הארצות אשר הדיחם שמה והשבתים על־אדמתם אשר נתתי
לאבותם:

		C'	C		C'	C
Type I:	2. (vs. 14)	X	X	4. (vs. 15)	X	X
	2. (vs. 15)	X	X	6. (vs. 11)	X	X
	3. (vs. 11)	X	X	6. (vs. 13)	X	X
Type II:	43. (vs. 14)	X	X	47. (vs. 4)	X*	X*
Type III:	52. (vs. 15)	X	X	54. (vs. 12)	X	X
	53. (vs. 4)	-	Xc	60. (vv. 10f.)	X	X
Type IV:	68. (vs. 9)	-	Xc	78. (vs. 9)	X	X
	(69. (vs. 4)	X*	X*	85. (vs. 4)	X	X
				85. (vs. 6)	-	Xc

Summary Tabulation of Instances

	I	II	III	IV	totals
C':	6	2	3	3	14
C+:	-	-	1	2	3
C:	6	2	4	5	17

Although Mowinckel ascribed this passage to his A source, many subsequent scholars have assigned it to the Deuteronomistic C corpus on the basis of its theological *Tendenz*, characteristic diction, prose style, and literary form.[36] The diction is especially evident in vv. 4, 9, and 10ff. With respect to theology, this section, as is common for C passages throughout the book, describes the imminent desolation of Judah and provides an explanation; destruction and exile seem to be unavoidable, and they are the direct consequences of the widespread apostasy from Yahweh. "Because they served foreign gods [in their native land], they will have to serve foreign gods in exile."[37] Accordingly, Hyatt has posited that

---

[36]For example, Leslie, *Jeremiah* (New York: Abingdon Press, 1954), pp. 88f., 292; Rudolph, *Jeremia,* pp. 93-95.

vv. 10-13 (as well as 5:18-19; 22:8-9; 9:12-16) were designed "to give a ready explanation for the desolation of Judah in 587 B.C. written after Nebuchadnezzar's invasion and his capture of Jerusalem."[38] In addition to the linguistic and theological indicators of C, Janssen[39] and Nicholson[40] have identified in this prose narrative literary structures which occur elsewhere in the C material and the Dtr corpus. Janssen has seen in 16:1ff. (as well as chapters 7, 11, 17:19-27, 18, 21, 22, 25, 34 and 35) a structural/formal pattern which is virtually identical to that of at least six prose discourses in Dtr.[41] Nicholson has focused instead on vv. 10-13 (and 5:19; 9:11b-15; 22:8-9). Here he has seen a structure which corresponds with that of two passages in the Deuteronomic and Deuteronomistic literature (Deut 29:21-27 and 1 Kgs 9:8-9), having three main parts:

  i. the question
  ii. the answer and explanation
  iii. a restatement of the circumstances which prompted the question.[42]

Most of the characteristic features of the C material are represented fully in C'. In vv. 4, 6 and 9, C+ has taken phrases which already appear in the text and turned them into formulaic language by modest additions. In vs. 4, the texts diverge in their images of destruction, and C' lacks some of the Deuteronomic diction to be found in C. Apart from these minor discrepancies, the C features are fully represented in C' as in C.

17:19-27

The passage is represented in the two traditions without significant variations. A few minor variants may be observed below (e.g., vv. 19, 20, 23 [OG plus], 27). It is impossible to ascertain whether an autobiographical

---

[37]Rudolph, *Jeremia*, p. 95.

[38]Hyatt, "Deuteronomic Edition," p. 80.

[39]Janssen, *Exilszeit*, pp. 105ff.

[40]Nicholson, *Preaching*, pp. 59ff.

[41]See pp. 23-25 above.

[42]Nicholson, *Preaching*, p. 61; he has identified this literary structure also in the Annals of Asshurbanapal as well as in biblical passages outside the Deuteronomic and Deuteronomistic corpora (Ex 7:26f., 13:14a-15b; Josh 4:6-7b, 21-24).

account lies behind this narrative (as the MT implies), since "to me" (אלי
in vs. 19) is present only in the expanded text.

(19) כה-אמר יהוה אלי הלך ועמדת בשער בני-עם^x אשר
יבאו בו מלכי יהודה ואשר יצאו בו ובכל שערי ירושלם:
(20) ואמרת אליהם שמעו דבר-יהוה מלכי יהודה וכל-
יהודה וכל ישבי ירושלם הבאים בשערים האלה: (21)
כה אמר יהוה השמרו בנפשותיכם^x ואל-תשאו משא ביום
השבת והבאתם^x בשערי ירושלם: (22) ולא-תוציאו משא
מבתיכם ביום השבת וכל-מלאכה לא תעשו וקדשתם את-
יום השבת כאשר צויתי את-אבותיכם: (23) ולא שמעו
ולא הטו את-אזנם ויקשו את-ערפם¹ לבלתי שומע^x
ולבלתי קחת מוסר: (24) והיה אם-שמע תשמעון אלי
נאם-יהוה לבלתי הביא משא בשערי העיר הזאת ביום
השבת ולקדש את-יום השבת לבלתי עשות-בה^x כל-מלאכה:
(25) ובאו בשערי העיר הזאת מלכים ושרים ישבים על-
כסא דוד רכבים¹ ברכב^x ובסוסים המה ושריהם איש
יהודה וישבי ירושלם וישבה העיר-הזאת לעולם:(26)
ובאו מערי-יהודה ומסביבות ירושלם ומארץ בנימן ומן-
ההר^x ומן-הנגב מבאים עולה וזבח ומנחה ולבונה
ומבאי תודה בית יהוה: (27) ואם^x-לא תשמעו אלי
לקדש את-יום השבת ולבלתי שאת משא^x ובא בשערי
ירושלם ביום השבת והצתי אש בשעריה ואכלה ארמנות^x
ירושלם ולא תכבה:

		C'	C			C'	C
Type I:	36. (vs. 21)	X	X				
Type II:	41. (vs. 25)	X	X	46. (vs. 23)		X	X
Type IV:	72. (vs. 23)	X	X	83. (vs. 20)		X	X
	79. (vs. 23)	X	X	88. (vs. 25)		X	X
				92. (vs. 25)		X	X

---

[1]OG adds *huper tous pateras autōn*.

Summary Tabulation of Instances

	I	II	III	IV	totals
C':	1	2	-	5	8
C+:	-	-	-	-	-
C:	1	2	-	5	8

Since Kuenen,[43] the majority of commentators have assigned 17:19-27
to the post-exilic period (around the time of Ezra) owing to its marked
emphasis on Sabbath observance (cf. Neh 13:15-22). This late ascription,
however, has been challenged by several more recent critics who date the
passage in the exilic period and argue for its inclusion in the Deuteronomistic C source (or its equivalent).[44] Their judgment is based on the
passage's diction (Rudolph and Hyatt), structure (Janssen and Nicholson),
style (Leslie, Rudolph and Hyatt), and theology (to a certain extent, all
the above). The relevant diction is distributed sparsely throughout the
text, however, and 63 percent of the indexed words and phrases which do
occur are unattested in either Dt or Dtr. The passage's diffuseness, verbosity (vv. 21b-22, 24 and 27), and use of rhetoric (vs. 21a, cf. Deut 4:15
and Josh 23:11) are characteristic of the C corpus as a whole, and many
have regarded this as evidence of its association with Dtr. Arguments
from form have been advanced as well. Thiel has described 17:19-27 as an
alternative sermon (introduction 19aα, Yahweh's commissioning the
prophet in vv. 19aβ-20aα, the mandate to hear in vs. 20aβb, the messenger formula in the imperative in vv. 21f., a survey of the past [the disobedience of the fathers] in vv. 22bβ, 23, alternative I in vs. 24 and the
promise of salvation in vv. 25f., alternative II in vs. 27a and the threat of
judgment in vs. 27b).[45] Nicholson has argued that 17:19-27 is based on a
covenant form which is frequently employed by Deuteronomic and

---

[43]A Kuenen, *Historisch-kritische Einleitung in die Bücher des Alten
Testament*, II: *Die prophetischen Bücher*, 1892.

[44]Rudolph, *Jeremia*, pp. 101ff.; Leslie, *Jeremiah*, pp. 316f.; Hyatt,
"Deuteronomic Edition," p. 82; Herrmann, *Heilserwartungen*, pp. 172ff.;
Nicholson, *Preaching*, pp. 65f., 124f.; Thiel, *Die deuteronomistische
Redaktion*, 1-25, pp. 203ff.

[45]Thiel, *Die deuteronomistische Redaktion*, 1-25, p. 204; Herrmann has
also examined this *Stilform* and found that here as elsewhere (12:14-17;
18:7-10; 24:1ff.) salvation and destruction stand side by side as two possibilities for the fate of the people of God (*Heilserwartungen*, pp. 174ff).

Deuteronomistic authors. The basic structure of this form varies in the following way: for Deuteronomic and Deuteronomistic passages outside of Jeremiah, (1) introduction, (2) historical retrospect and/or hortatory prologue, (3) Yahweh's call to obedience, and (4) blessings and curses; for those Deuteronomistic passages in the book of Jeremiah, (1) introduction, vv. 19f., (2) Yahweh's call to obedience, vv. 21f., (3) description of Israel's apostasy and disobedience, vs. 23, and (4) the pronouncement of judgment, vv. 24-27.

Most commentators agree that 17:19-27 in its present form is incompatible with, or at least dissimilar to, the theological ideas and concerns expressed in the poetic oracles of the prophet, and that it is consistent instead with many motifs which recur in Dtr literature. Nicholson, for example, has argued that its call for obedience to the Law—an index of Dtr theology—is a link with the Deuteronomistic literary corpus. For Thiel its survey of the past is Deuteronomistic in outlook; the retrospect of Israel's historical experience as the people of God shows only its hard-heartedness and disobedience to Yahweh's word. Bright has found the theological ideas and concerns expressed in 17:19-27 to be entirely congruent with Dtr's conviction that the exile had resulted from breach of law and covenant, of which Sabbath observance was an integral part. Accordingly, he contends that the present passage "is no more than a development of good Deuteronomic theology. In short, it leads us into the world of Dtr and Dtr is quite enough to account for it."[46] For Rudolph, this section reflects a central motif of Dtr, namely the prophetic warning serving to heighten the awareness that the covenant people had brought the catastrophe of 587 upon themselves (vs. 27). Although the threat of judgment had already been fulfilled, the promise (vv. 25f.) still remained a future possibility if the people would but heed the warning of the prophet.[47]

Since the texts show little divergence, all of these observations are as appropriate to C' as they are to C.

18:1-12

As is often the case, the MT plusses do not significantly alter the meaning of the passage; instead they provide pronominal suffixes (e.g.,

---

[46]J. Bright, "The Date of the Prose Sermons," p. 23.

[47]Rudolph, *Jeremia,* pp. 102f.

vs. 4), various formulae (vv. 6, 11), and substantives and relative clauses which serve in general to make the text more explicit.

(2) הַדָּבָר אֲשֶׁר הָיָה אֶל־יִרְמְיָהוּ מֵאֵת יְהוָה לֵאמֹר: (1)
(3) קוּם וְיָרַדְתָּ בֵּית הַיּוֹצֵר וְשָׁמָּה אַשְׁמִיעֲךָ^X אֶת־דְּבָרָי:
(4) וָאֵרֵד בֵּית הַיּוֹצֵר וְהִנֵּהוּ עֹשֶׂה מְלָאכָה עַל־הָאָבְנָיִם:
וְנִשְׁחַת הַכְּלִי אֲשֶׁר הוּא עֹשֶׂה בַּחֹמֶר ¹ בְּיַד הַיּוֹצֵר¹ וְשָׁב
וַיַּעֲשֵׂהוּ^X כְּלִי אַחֵר כַּאֲשֶׁר יָשַׁר ²בְּעֵינֵי הַיּוֹצֵר² לַעֲשׂוֹת:
(5) וַיְהִי דְבַר־יְהוָה אֵלַי לֵאמֹר: (6) הֲכַיּוֹצֵר הַזֶּה
לֹא־אוּכַל לַעֲשׂוֹת לָכֶם בֵּית יִשְׂרָאֵל נְאֻם יְהוָה הִנֵּה כַחֹמֶר
בְּיַד הַיּוֹצֵר כֵּן־אַתֶּם^X בְּיָדִי בֵּית יִשְׂרָאֵל: (7) רֶגַע אֲדַבֵּר
עַל־גּוֹי וְעַל מַמְלָכָה לִנְתוֹשׁ וְלִנְתוֹץ³ וּלְהַאֲבִיד^X: (8)
וְשָׁב הַגּוֹי הַהוּא מֵרָעָתוֹ^X אֲשֶׁר דִּבַּרְתִּי עָלָיו וְנִחַמְתִּי עַל־
הָרָעָה אֲשֶׁר חָשַׁבְתִּי לַעֲשׂוֹת לוֹ^X: (9) וְרֶגַע אֲדַבֵּר עַל־
גּוֹי וְעַל־מַמְלָכָה לִבְנֹת וְלִנְטֹעַ: (10) וְעָשָׂה^X הָרָעָה בְּעֵינַי
לְבִלְתִּי שְׁמֹעַ בְּקוֹלִי וְנִחַמְתִּי עַל־הַטּוֹבָה אֲשֶׁר אָמַרְתִּי
לְהֵיטִיב^X אוֹתוֹ^X: (11) וְעַתָּה אֱמָר־נָא^X אֶל־אִישׁ־יְהוּדָה
וְעַל־יוֹשְׁבֵי יְרוּשָׁלִַם לֵאמֹר כֹּה אָמַר יְהוָה הִנֵּה אָנֹכִי
יוֹצֵר עֲלֵיכֶם רָעָה וְחֹשֵׁב עֲלֵיכֶם מַחֲשָׁבָה שׁוּבוּ^X נָא אִישׁ
מִדַּרְכּוֹ הָרָעָה וְהֵיטִיבוּ דַרְכֵיכֶם וּמַעַלְלֵיכֶם: (12) וְאָמְרוּ
נוֹאָשׁ כִּי־אַחֲרֵי מַחְשְׁבוֹתֵינוּ נֵלֵךְ וְאִישׁ שְׁרִרוּת לִבּוֹ־
הָרָע נַעֲשֶׂה:

		C'	C		C'	C
Type I:	1. (vs. 10)	X	X	12. (vs. 11)	X	X
	9. (vs. 10)	X	X			
Type II:	41. (vs. 11)	X	X			
Type IV:	71. (vs. 1)	X	X	86. (vs. 9)	X	X
	82. (vs. 11)	–	Xc	91. (vs. 8)	–	Xc
	86. (vs. 7)	X	X			

---

¹OG reads *en tais chersin autou*.

²OG reads *enōpion autou*.

³May be absent in OG by haplography.

Summary Tabulation of Instances

	I	II	III	IV	totals
C':	3	1	-	3	7
C+:	-	-	-	2	2
C:	3	1	-	5	9

The text begins with the customary introductory sentence הדבר אשר
היה אל-ירמיהו מאת יהוה ("The word which came [lit. was] to Jeremiah
from Yahweh"). The autobiographical account which follows is in the
familiar rhetorical style. The diction we have indexed is distributed
unevenly; apart from the introductory formula, all the instances are in
vv. 7-11. The alternative speech form also appears in this section of the
passage (vv. 7f. and 9f.): here it emphasizes Yahweh's freedom to respond
to what a nation does, whether he has previously announced an intention
to do it harm or good. This explains why Israel can come to grief in spite
of his previous declaration of good; but it also means (vs. 11) that the evil
he now intends can be avoided if the people "turn away" (שוב) from their
wrongdoing. In the last verse, however, the people are said to refuse to
change their ways (vs. 12). Nicholson has argued that the possibility of
salvation formulated in the text, with its appeal to "turn again" (vv. 8,
11b), is a direct expression of the Deuteronomistic kerygma which offers
Yahweh's restoration and blessing in response to the people's "turning
again."[48] As for theology, the text is full of Deuteronomistic ideas,
especially in vv. 7-12.[49] In this respect, Hyatt has suggested that a Deuteronomistic editor gave his own pessimistic interpretation in vv. 7-12 of
a parable which was evidently optimistic in its original form (vv. 1-6); the
editor has transformed the original emphasis on the sovereignty of Yahweh over Israel (vs. 6) by making the "fate of the people depend upon what

---

[48]Nicholson, *Preaching,* p. 80.

[49]See, for example, Mowinckel, *Komposition,* p. 31; Rudolph, *Jeremia,*
pp. 103ff.; Herrmann, *Heilserwartungen,* pp. 162ff.; Hyatt, "Deuteronomic
Edition," pp. 82f.; Thiel, *Die deuteronomistische Redaktion,* 1-25, pp.
210ff.; Skinner, *Prophecy and Religion: Studies in the Life of Jeremiah*
(Cambridge: University Press, 1922), p. 163; Skinner argues there that
vv. 7-10 are "the well-meant homily of an over-zealous commentator."

they do, not God."[50] Hyatt also finds D's fundamental doctrine of divine retribution" set forth clearly in vv. 7-12.[51]

Most of the characteristic C features are fully represented in C'. C+ has, however, filled out two phrases in C' to produce idiomatic diction in C (MT) (vv. 8, 11; cf. 7).

19:2b-9, 11b-13

These verses have been treated separately in this study in accordance with the vast majority of exegetes who have come to regard them as intrusive. It was Giesebrecht who first argued that vv. 3-9, 11b-13 were inserted into an original account, probably written by Baruch, which presently comprises the remainder of 19:1-20:6.[52] That these verses are a self-contained unit is evident from their underlying structure: (1) an introductory word to hear the prophetic message in vv. 2b-3, (2) an accusation in vv. 4f., and (3) an announcement of judgment upon the cultic site of Topheth, Tal Hinnom, and upon Jerusalem itself in vv. 6-9, 11b-13.[53] It is interesting to note that the narrative continuity between vv. 2b-9 and vv. 12-13 in the OG is slightly disturbed in the MT by the words, generally recognized as intrusive, in vs. 11b (C+).[54]

Overall the MT and OG *Vorlage* are very close. There are, however, a few quantitative variants (vv. 3, 5, 9, 11b), the longest of which occurs in vs. 11b. None of these variants alter the meaning of the text in a significant way. Although the conjunctive *wāw* in vs. 4 is not represented in the Greek translation, no certain judgment about the *Vorlage* is possible. By employing the conjunction here the MT begins a new clause with ומלאו, and places ומלכי יהודה with the preceding clause. Finally, it may be observed that there are several OG plusses in the passage (vv. 2b, 3 [twice], 7).

---

[50]Hyatt, "Deuteronomic Edition," p. 83.

[51]Ibid.

[52]F. Giesebrecht, *Das Buch Jeremia,* Handkommentar zum Alten Testament III. 2, 2d ed. (Göttingen: Vandenhoeck and Ruprecht, 1907), pp. 109-13.

[53]Thiel, *Die deuteronomistische Redaktion,* 1-25, pp. 219ff.

[54]For example, Janzen, *Studies,* p. 43.

(2) וקראת שם את[x]־הדברים אשר־אדבר אליך: (3) ואמרת
שמעו דבר־יהוה מלכי יהודה[1] וישבי ירושלם[2] כה־אמר יהוה
צבאות אלהי ישראל הנני מביא[3]רעה על־המקום הזה[3] אשר
כל־שמעה תצלנה אזניו: (4) יען אשר עזבני וינכרו את־
המקום הזה ויקטרו־בו לאלהים אחרים אשר לא־ידעום המה
ואבתיהם ומלכי יהודה ומלאו[x] את־המקום הזה דם נקים:
(5) ובנו את־במות הבעל לשרף את־בניהם באש עלות
לבעל אשר לא־צויתי ולא דברתי ולא עלתה על[x]־לבי: (6)
לכן הנה־ימים באים נאם־יהוה ולא יקרא למקום הזה
עוד התפת וגיא בן־הנם כי אם־גיא ההרגה: (7) ובקתי[x]
את־עצת יהודה[x] וירושלם במקום הזה והפלתים בחרב
לפני איביהם וביד מבקשי נפשם ונתתי את־נבלתם למאכל
לעוף השמים ולבהמת הארץ: (8) ושמתי את־העיר הזאת
לשמה ולשרקה כל עבר עליה ישם וישרק על־כל־מכתה:
(9) והאכלתים[x] את־בשר בניהם ואת בשר בנתיהם ואיש
בשר־רעהו יאכלו במצור ובמצוק אשר יציקו להם
איביהם ומבקשי נפשם: (11) ובחפת יקברו מאין מקום
לקבר (12) כן־אעשה[4]למקום הזה נאם־יהוה[4] וליושביו[x]
ולתת[x] את־העיר הזאת כתפת: (13) והיו[x] בתי ירושלם
ובתי מלכי יהודה כמקום התפת הטמאים לכל[x] הבתים
אשר קטרו על־גנתיהם לכל צבא השמים והסך נסכים לאלהים
אחרים:

		C'	C		C'	C
Type I:	10. (vs. 3)	X	X	13. (vs. 4)	X	X
Type II:	38. (vs. 4)	X	X	43. (vs. 6)	X	X
	39. (vs. 8)	X	X	49. (vs. 3)	X	X
Type III:	53. (vs. 7)	X	X	55. (vs. 4)	X	X
				62. (vs. 9)	X	X

---

[1]OG adds *kai andres Iouda*.

[2]OG adds *kai hoi eisporeuomenoi en tais pulais tautais*.

[3]Transposed in OG.

[4]Transposed in OG.

Type IV:	68. (vs. 3)	-	Xc	77. (vs. 9)	-	X
	77. (vs. 7)	X	X	84. (vs. 5)	X	X

Indices attested only in OG *Vorlage*

Type II:	41
Type IV:	83

Summary Tabulation of Instances

	I	II	III	IV	totals
C':	2	4	3	2	11
C+:	-	-	-	2	2
C:	2	4	3	4	13

In addition to the sermonic prose style, many of the phrases and theo-logical ideas and concerns which appear in this passage are characteristic of the C corpus and akin to Deuteronomic tradition. All of the diction we have indexed occurs in vv. 3-9. Nine of the thirteen instances in the MT (C) are stock phrases from Deuteronomy or Dtr, whereas only four are peculiar to the Jeremianic prose sermons. Verses 5-7 correspond very closely to the judgment sermon in Jer 7:31-33 and reproduce several of its idioms verbatim. As for its theological ideas and concerns, several themes are clearly Deuteronomistic. It emphasizes the existence of the sin of Topheth in the valley of Hinnom, "which was a symbol to the Deuterono-mists of the worst heresy of Manasseh,"[55] and of the detestable cultic rite of child sacrifice. This abominable practice, associated with the ill-fated reign of Manasseh—the most deplorable king of Judah's history in the opinion of the Deuteronomists—had apparently erupted anew in the land of Judah. In the judgment of the Deuteronomists, "it was the awful horror of the child sacrifice which was bringing about the downfall of the Judean state in terrible catastrophe . . . ; it was the sin of sins in Judah."[56] Thus the message of the "sermon on Topheth" is identical to other passages in the C corpus, namely that Judah had brought divine judgment upon itself by its abominable cultic rites and its rejection of Yahweh's word.

---

[55]Hyatt, "Jeremiah and Deuteronomy," p. 167.

[56]Leslie, *Jeremiah*, p. 319.

Only two of the thirteen instances of C diction are not found in C', and other characteristic features of C (style and theology) are fully represented. In vs. 3, plusses in the OG *Vorlage* create two additional instances of C diction; these are the only occasions where the OG employs C phrases that are absent in the MT (C).

21:1-10

The OG *Vorlage* is shorter than the MT by 12 percent (or twenty-one words). The MT plusses do not introduce significant changes. They add personal names and titles (vv. 2, 4, 7), stock phrases (vv. 5, 9), a divine epithet and an oracular formula (vv. 4, 10) and explicate the sense of the text (e.g., vv. 4, 7). This does, however, introduce a new idea in vs. 7 by alluding explicitly to the king of Babylon, Nebuchadnezzar, as the instrument of Yahweh's punishment, while the OG *Vorlage* states only in general terms that Zedekiah and his entourage will be delivered into the possession of *their enemies.* In fact the OG *Vorlage* never mentions Nebuchadnezzar by name (cf. vs. 2). Moreover, the MT refers to both the king of Babylon and the Chaldeans invading Palestine (vs. 4), whereas the *Vorlage* of the LXX mentions only the latter.

(1) הדבר אשר־היה אל־ירמיהו מאת יהוה בשלח אליו
המלך צדקיהו את־פשחור בן־מלכיה ואת־צפניה בן־
מעשיה הכהן לאמר: (2) דרש־נא^x בעדנו את־יהוה כי
נבוכדראצר מלך־בבל נלחם עלינו אולי יעשה יהוה
אותנו ככל־נפלאתיו ויעלה מעלינו: (3) ויאמר ירמיהו
אליהם כה תאמרן אל־צדקיהו¹: (4) כה־אמר יהוה אלהי
ישראל הנני מסב את־כלי המלחמה אשר בידכם אשר אתם
נלחמים בם את־מלך בבל ואת־הכשדים הצרים עליכם^x
מחוץ לחומה ואספתי אותם אל־תוך העיר הזאת: (5)
ונלחמתי אני אתכם ביד נטויה ובזרוע חזקה ובאף
ובחמה ובקצף גדול: (6) והכיתי ^xאת־יושבי העיר^x
הזאת ואת־האדם^x ואת־הבהמה בדבר גדול ימתו^x:
(7) ואחרי־כן נאם־יהוה אתן את־צדקיהו מלך־יהודה
ואת־עבדיו ואת־העם ואת^x־הנשארים בעיר הזאת מן־
הדבר מן־²החרב ומן־הרעב² ביד נבוכדראצר מלך־

---

[1]OG adds *basilea Iouda.*
[2]Transposed in OG.

בכל וביד איביהם וביד מבקשי נפשם והכם לפי-חרב
לא-יחום‎ˣ עליהם ולא יחמל ולא ירחם: (8) ואל-
העם הזה תאמר כה אמר יהוה הנני נתן לפניכם את-
דרך החיים ואת-דרך המות: (9) הישב בעיר הזאת
ימות בחרב וברעב ובדבר והיוצא ונפל על-הכשדים
הצרים עליכם יחיה והיתה-לו‎ˣ נפשו לשלל:³ (10)
כי שמתי פני בעיר‎ˣ הזאת לרעה ולא לטובה נאם-
יהוה ביד-מלך בבל תנתן ושרפה באש:

		C'	C			C'	C
Type I:	18. (vs. 5)	X	X				
Type III:	57. (vs. 5)	-	Xc	64. (vs. 8)		X	X
Type IV:	69. (vs. 7)	X	X	71. (vs. 1)		X	X
	69. (vs. 9)	-	Xc	73. (vs. 6)		X	X
				77. (vs. 7)		X	X

Summary Tabulation of Instances

	I	II	III	IV	totals
C':	1	-	1	4	6
C+:	-	-	1	1	2
C:	1	-	2	5	8

The diction, style, and (to a lesser extent) ideology (which is admittedly
not altogether inconsistent with the biographical accounts of the prophet)
of this passage have been regarded as characteristic of the Deuteronomistic C material. The narrative begins with the conventional introductory
formula (vs. 1a), and it exhibits the verbose style (especially in vv. 4, 7)
and alternative speech form (vv. 8f.) which are frequently employed in
other C passages. With the exception of the introductory sentence, all of
the diction we have indexed is found in vv. 5-9. Scholars generally con-
cede, however, that this passage deviates at points from other C materials in the book. Mowinckel discerned a rhythmic and poetic dimension
which sets 21:1-10 apart from the customary prose sermon of the C
corpus. Thiel has noted that vv. 1b-3 are written in the biographical style

---

³OG adds *kai zēsetai.*

of Baruch's memoirs without a trace of the usual Deuteronomistic diction.[57] Accordingly, it has been argued that the author has reworked a section of the stock of biographical traditions written by Baruch. Hyatt and others have suggested that 21:1ff. is a Deuteronomistic "rewriting of the incident which is more accurately reported in chapter 37 . . . ,"[58] its secondary and artifical construction indicated by its abrupt change of address from Zedekiah in vv. 3-7 to the general populace in vv. 8-10.[59]

Six of the eight instances of indexed diction which appear in C are present intact in C'. Two phrases in C' have been filled out by C+ to form standard clichés. With reference to the first (vs. 5), Janzen has observed that the "M elsewhere fills out אף secondarily behind חמה (42:18), and may be doing the same here."[60] The second (vs. 9) occurs (in full) fifteen times in the MT of Jeremiah but only eight times in the OG *Vorlage*.[61] In addition, Rudolph's characterization of vv. 4 and 7 as extremely verbose is not really applicable to the shorter text of C'.

22:1-5

The MT and OG *Vorlage* are virtually identical. In vs. 1 πορευου και is an OG plus, and in vs. 2 there is an apparent content variant; other differences between the MT and OG involve matters which cannot really be controlled.

כה אמר יהוה[1] רד בית־מלך יהודה ודברת שם את־ (1)
הדבר הזה: (2) ואמרת שמע דבר־יהוה מלך יהודה הישב
על־כסא דוד אתם ועבדיך[2] ועמך הבאים[X] בשערים האלה:
(3) כה אמר יהוה עשו משפט וצדקה והצילו גזול מיד
עשוק[X] וגר יתום[X] ואלמנה אל־תנו אל־[X]־תחמסו ודם נקי
אל־ושפכו במקום הזה: (4) כי אם־עשו תעשו את־הדבר
הזה ובאו בשערי הבית הזה מלכים ישבים לדוד[X] על־כסאו[X]
רכבים ברכב ובסוסים[X] הוא[X] ועבדו[X] ועמו[X]: (5) ואם

---

[57] Thiel, *Die deuteronomistische Redaktion, 1-25*, p. 233.
[58] Hyatt, "Deuteronomic Edition," pp. 83f.
[59] Ibid., p. 84.
[60] Janzen, *Studies*, p. 43.
[61] Ibid., pp. 43f., 205.

[1] OG adds *poreuou kai*.
[2] OG adds *kai ho oikos*.

לא תשמעו^x את-הדברים האלה בי נשבעתי נאם-יהוה כי—
לחרבה יהיה הבית הזה:

		C'	C			C'	C
Type I:	13. (vs. 3)	X	X				
Type III:	58. (vs. 3)	X	X				
Type IV:	83. (vs. 2)	X	X	92. (vs. 4)		X	X

Summary Tabulation of Instances

	I	II	III	IV	totals
C':	1	-	1	2	4
C+:	-	-	-	-	-
C:	1	-	1	2	4

This brief passage has been included among the Deuteronomistic C materials on the basis of its diction and theological ideas. The passage presupposes that the continuation of the Davidic dynasty is contingent upon the king's obedience to the Law (1 Kgs 2:1-4, 9:4ff.; cf. Deut 17:18ff.; 2 Kgs 21:1ff).[62] Moreover, it depicts the prophet as preacher of the Law, who offers the monarch and his entourage (in an alternative speech form) the choice of blessing for obedience (vs. 4) or judgment in case of disobedience (vs. 5). Finally, "the conventional and general tone of the admonitions in vss. 2-5"[63] and the materialistic nature of the promises are said to indicate an association with Deuteronomistic tradition.

All of the characteristic features of the C corpus are represented fully in C'.

25:1-14

The text traditions differ in several respects. First, the OG *Vorlage* is much shorter; it lacks seventy words present in the MT, which is 29 percent of the text. The MT plusses take the form of short additions which

---

[62]Nicholson, *Preaching*, pp. 86ff.

[63]Hyatt, *Jeremiah*, p. 980.

serve to clarify or accentuate the text (e.g., vv. 2, 3, 4, 9, 11), or long
additions which either introduce new subject matter (e.g., vv. 1b, 9, 12,
14) or repeat already present material (e.g., 7b from vs. 6b). Second, the
MT and the OG *Vorlage* disagree in their identification of the speaker in
vv. 3-4. The latter consistently presents the whole of vv. 3-7 as an oracular form of prophetic speech in which the "I" is Yahweh who speaks
throughout in the first person. In the MT, however, the "I" in vs. 3 is
Jeremiah who speaks vv. 3-4, and Yahweh is referred to in the third
person; then in vv. 5-7 the prophet cites the words of Yahweh, although
Yahweh is still referred to in the third person until the end of vs. 6. Third,
in the OG *Vorlage* the passage (which ends with vs. 13a) is predominantly
a threat of destruction against "the people of Judah and the inhabitants of
Jerusalem." In the MT's version of this passage this threat of destruction
is eclipsed by a fuller prediction of salvation (vs. 14). Hyatt has suggested
that the more detailed prophecy of salvation in the MT (vv. 11ff.) was
intended to "soften the threat against Judah . . . after the Babylonian
exile was over, or near the end of the exile."[64] Lastly, the texts diverge
in their reference to the instruments of Yahweh's punishment upon Judah.
In the MT these include "Nebuchadrezzar, the king of Babylon, my servant" (vs. 9), and coming judgment is announced upon "the king of Babylon
and that nation, the land of the Chaldaeans" (vs. 12). The OG *Vorlage*
lacks these specific references; it describes Yahweh's coming judgment in
entirely general terms, mentioning only a "tribe from the north"(משפחה
מצוון /πατριαν απο βορρα). By all indications the texts have undergone a
very complicated process of transmission. It is generally agreed (even
among scholars who usually prefer the MT over the OG or who take a
neutral position) that the OG represents a form of text which is much
closer to the original than that preserved by the MT (e.g., Hyatt, Bright,
Thiel, et al.).

(1) הדבר אשר-היה על^x-ירמיהו על-כל-עם יהודה
בשנה הרבעית ליהויקים בן-יאשיהו מלך יהודה היא
השנה הראשנית לנבוכדראצר מלך בבל: (2) אשר דבר
ירמיהו הנביא על-כל-עם יהודה ואל כל-ישבי ירושלם
לאמר: (3) מן^x-שלש עשרה שנה ליאשיהו בן-אמון מלך
יהודה ועד היום הזה זה¹ שלש ועשרים שנה היה דבר-

_____

[64]Ibid., p. 999.

יהוה אלי ואדבר אליכם אשכים^x ודבר ולא שמעתם: (4)

ושלח יהוה² אליכם את-כל-עבדיו^x הנבאים השכם ושלח^x

ולא שמעתם ולא-הטיתם את-אזנכם לשמע: (5) לאמר שובו-

נא איש מדרכו הרעה ומרע מעלליכם ושבו על-האדמה אשר

נתן יהוה³ לכם ולאבותיכם למן-עולם ועד-עולם: (6)

ואל-תלכו אחרי אלהים אחרים לעבדם ולהשתחות להם

ולא-תכעיסו אותי במעשה ידיכם ולא ארע לכם: (7) ולא-

שמעתם אלי נאם-יהוה למען הכעסוני במעשה ידיכם לרע

לכם: (8) לכן כה אמר יהוה צבאות יען אשר לא-שמעתם^x

את-דברי: (9) הנני שלח ולקחתי את-כל-⁴משפחות צפון⁴

נאם-יהוה ואל-נבוכדראצר מלך-בבל עבדי והבאתים על-

הארץ הזאת ועל-ישביה ועל כל-הגוים האלה סביב^x

והחרמתים ושמתים לשמה ולשרקה ולחרבת^x עולם: (10)

והאבדתי מהם קול ששון וקול שמחה קול חתן וקול כלה

קול^x רחים^x ואור נר: (11) והיתה כל-הארץ הזאת

לחרבה לשמה ועבדו הגוים האלה את-מלך בבל שבעים

שנה: (12) והיה כמלאות^x שבעים שנה אפקד על-מלך-

בבל ועל-הגוי ההוא נאם-יהוה את-עונם ועל-ארץ

כשדים ושמתי אתו לשממות עולם: (13) והבאיתי על-

הארץ ההיא את-כל-דברי אשר-דברתי עליה את כל-הכתוב

בספר הזה אשר נבא ירמיהו על-כל-הגוים: (14) כי עבדו-

בם גם-המה גוים רבים ומלכים גדולים ושלמתי להם

כפעלם וכמעשה ידיהם:

		C'	C		C'	C
Type I:	3. (vs. 6)	X	X	6. (vs. 6)	X	X
	4. (vs. 5)	X	X	8. (vs. 6)	X	X
	5. (vs. 4)	X	X	8. (vs. 7)	-	X
				12. (vs. 5)	X	X
Type II:	39. (vs. 9)	X	X	39. (vs. 11)	X	X
Type III:	63. (vs. 5)	X	X			

---

[1]Omitted in OG perhaps by haplography.

[2]OG reads *kai apestellon*.

[3]OG reads *edōka*.

[4]OG reads *patrian apo borra*.

Type IV:	70. (vs. 3)	X	X	76. (vs. 12)	-	Xc
	70. (vs. 4)	X	X	78. (vs. 10)	X	X
	72. (vs. 4)	X	X	81. (vs. 14)	-	X
				90. (vs. 9)	-	X

Summary Tabulation of Instances

	I	II	III	IV	totals
C':	6	2	1	4	13
C+:	1	-	-	3	4
C:	7	2	1	7	17

As is customary for C passages, 25:1-14 employs several phrases from the Deuteronomistic tradition as well as from its own stock of clichés. A high percentage of the diction we have indexed occurs in vv. 4-7 (11 of 17, or 65 percent). In addition, the text shows a fondness for repetition, rhetoric, and distinctively Deuteronomistic ideas. Regarding the latter, the passage (especially vv. 3-11) manifests a clear affinity with prophetic proclamation in Dtr (2 Kgs 17:13-18). As mentioned above,[65] this convention typically has three main parts: (1) the prophetic warning to heed Yahweh's word spoken by his servants, the prophets, vv. 4b-6; (2) a brief statement noting Israel's rejection of the prophetic word, vv. 4a, 7; and (3) an announcement of Yahweh's judgment as a result of Israel's rejection, vv. 8-11.[66] Like the message of the prophets in Dtr, Jeremiah is to "warn the people that, as the result of their constant refusal to heed the prophets sent by Yahweh, they were about to be destroyed . . . ."[67] It is also analogous to Dtr that the specific sin of the people, for which they are reprimanded, is their apostasy from Yahweh, that is, their worship of foreign gods (vs. 6). Together with eight other prose sermons in Jeremiah and several more in Deuteronomistic literature, the passage has been said to reflect a conventional structure analogous to ancient Near Eastern vassal treaties which finds its clearest expression in the biblical materials in the book of Deuteronomy.[68]

Thirteen of the seventeen instances of C diction we have identified are represented in C'. The remaining four are peculiar to C (C+), and of these three are stock C clichés which are unattested in Deuteronomy or the

---

[65] See pp. 24-25 above.

[66] Nicholson, *Preaching,* pp. 55ff.

[67] Hyatt, *Jeremiah,* p. 998.

[68] Nicholson, *Preaching,* pp. 32ff.

Deuteronomistic historical work (our Type IV); the fourth occurs in vs. 7b which is clearly a doublet of 6b.[69] The reference to Nebuchadrezzar as "my servant" (עבדי)—another standard C cliché—appears three times in the MT of Jeremiah (25:9; 27:6; 43:10) but not at all in the OG. Whether the absence of this idiom in the OG is due to the translator's theological bias (so Graf, Volz, Rudolph, Bright, et al.) or is in fact indicative of the OG *Vorlage* (Tov and Janzen) cannot be determined with certainty, but in view of the MT's general *Tendenz* in this chapter "to make more explicit the identity of Judah's impending foe," as well as its "syntactic awkwardness,"[70] the latter is more probable.

27:1-22

In his article, "Exegetical Notes on the Hebrew *Vorlage* of the LXX of Jeremiah 27 (34),"[71] Tov has reconstructed the Hebrew text underlying the LXX of Jer 34 (27) and has compared this with the MT, commenting on the nature and origin of the MT plusses.

The OG *Vorlage* of this chapter differs noticeably from the MT, the main difference being that the MT contains a "relatively large number of plusses over against the LXX . . . ."[72] In addition to comparably small expansions (e.g., the filling out of human names and titles [vs. 20 (twice)] and divine epithets [vv. 4, 18, 19] and inserting words for the sake of clarity and/or emphasis [vv. 5, 6, 8, 9, 10]), the MT contains several long plusses (vv. 1, 7, 13-14a, and the greater part of vv. 21f.). Altogether the MT is 42 percent (or 170 words) longer than the *Vorlage* of the OG.

(11) בראשית ממלכת יהויקם בן-יאושיהו מלך יהודה היה
הדבר הזה אל-ירמיה מאת יהוה לאמר: (2) כה-אמר יהוה
אלי עשה לך[x] מוסרות ומטות ונתתם[x] על-צוארך: (3)
ושלחתם אל-מלך אדום ואל-מלך מואב ואל-מלך[x] בני עמון ואל-
מלך צר ואל-מלך צידון ביד מלאכים[x] הבאים[1] ירושלם
אל-צדקיהו מלך יהודה: (4) וצוית אתם אל-אדניהם לאמר
כה-אמר יהוה צבאות אלהי ישראל כה תאמרו אל-אדניכם:

---

[69]Cf. Janzen, *Studies*, p. 13; Klein, *Textual Criticism*, p. 30.

[70]Janzen, *Studies*, p. 54.

[71]Tov, "Exegetical," pp. 79ff.

[72]Ibid., p. 77.

[1]OG adds *eis apantēsin autōn*.

‏(5) אנכי עשיתי את-הארץ את-האדם ואת-הבהמה אשר על-‏
‏פני הארץ בכחי הגדול ובזרעי הנטויה ונתתיה לאשר‏
‏ישר בעיני: (6) ועתה אנכי× נתתי את-כל-הארצות× האלה‏
‏ביד× נבוכדנאצר× מלך-בבל עבדי×² וגם את-חית השדה‏
‏נתתי·לו לעבדו: (7) ועבדו אתו כל-הגוים ואת-בנו‏
‏ואת-בן-בנו עד בא-עת ארצו גם-הוא ועבדו בו גוים‏
‏רבים ומלכים גדלים: (8) והיה הגוי והממלכה אשר‏
‏לא-יעבדו אתו את-נבוכדנאצר מלך-בבל ואת אשר לא-‏
‏יתן× את-צוארו× בעל מלך בבל בחרב וברעב ובדבר‏
‏אפקד על-הגוי³ ההוא נאם-יהוה עד-תמי אתם בידו:‏
‏(9) ואתם אל-תשמעו אל-נביאיכם ואל-קסמיכם ואל‏
‏חלמתיכם ואל-ענניכם ואל-כשפיכם אשר-הם אמרים‏
‏אליכם לאמר לא תעבדו את-מלך בבל: (10) כי שקר‏
‏הם נבאים לכם למען הרחיק אתכם מעל אדמתכם והדחתי‏
‏אתכם ואבדתם: (11) והגוי אשר יביא את-צוארו בעל‏
‏מלך-בבל ועבדו והנחתיו על-אדמתו נאם-יהוה ועבדה‏
‏וישב בה: (12) ואל-צדקיה מלך-יהודה דברתי ככל-‏
‏הדברים האלה לאמר הביאו את-צואריכם בעל מלך-בבל‏
‏ועבדו× אתו× ועמו וחיו: (13) למה תמותו אתה ועמך‏
‏בחרב ברעב ובדבר כאשר דבר יהוה אל-הגוי אשר לא-‏
‏יעבד את-מלך בבל: (14) ואל-תשמעו אל-דברי הנבאים‏
‏האמרים אליכם לאמר לא תעבדו את-מלך בבל כי שקר‏
‏הם נבאים לכם: (15) כי לא שלחתים נאם-יהוה והם‏
‏נבאים בשמי לשקר למען הדיחי× אתכם ואבדתם אתם‏
‏והנבאים הנבאים לכם⁴: (16) ואל-הכהנים ואל-כל-‏
‏העם הזה⁵ דברתי לאמר כה אמר יהוה אל-תשמעו אל-דברי‏
‏נביאיכם הנבאים לכם לאמר הנה כלי בית-יהוה מושבים‏
‏מבבלה עתה מהרה כי שקר המה נבאים לכם⁶: (17) אל-‏
‏תשמעו אליהם עבדו את-מלך-בבל וחיו למה תהיה העיר‏
‏הזאת חרבה: (18) ואם-נבאים הם ואם-יש דבר-יהוה אתם‏
‏יפגעו-נא× ⁷ביהוה צבאות⁷ לבלתי-באו הכלים הנותרים‏
‏בבית-יהוה ובית מלך יהודה ובירושלם בבלה: (19) כי‏
‏כה אמר יהוה צבאות אל-העמדים ועל-הים ועל-המכנות‏

---

²OG reads *douleuein autǭ*.

³OG reads *episkepsonmai autous*.

⁴OG adds *ep' adikǭ pseudē humin*.

⁵OG reads *kai panti tǭ laǭ toutǭ kai tois hiereusin*.

⁶OG adds *ouk apesteila autous*.

⁷OG reads simply *moi*.

ועל^x יתר הכלים הנותרים בעיר הזאת: (20) אשר לא-
לקחם^x נבוכדנאצר מלך בבל בגלותו^x את-יכוניה בן-
יהויקים מלך-יהודה מירושלם בבלה ואת כל-חרי יהודה
וירושלם: (21) כי כה אמר יהוה צבאות אלהי ישראל על-
הכלים הנותרים בית יהוה ובית מלך-יהודה וירושלם:
(22) בבלה יובאו ושמה יהיו עד יום פקדי אתם נאם-
יהוה והעליתים והשיבתים אל-המקום הזה:

		C'	C			C'	C
Type I:	39. (vs. 17)	-	X				
Type IV:	68. (vs. 4)	-	Xc	75. (vs. 14)	X	X
	68. (vs. 21)	-	X	75. (vs. 16)	X	X
	69. (vs. 8)	-	Xc	76. (vs. 8)	X	X
	69. (vs. 13)	-	X	80. (vs. 9)	X	X
	71. (vs. 1)	-	X *	80. (vs. 16)	X	X
	73. (vs. 5)	-	X	81. (vs. 7)	-	X
	75. (vs. 10)	X	X	90. (vs. 6)	-	X

Summary Tabulation of Instances

	I	II	III	IV	totals
C':	-	-	-	6	6
C+:	-	1	-	8	9
C:	-	1	-	14	15

With the notable exception of Rudolph, who argues for the authenticity of Jeremiah 27 and includes it in his A source, the majority of commentators have assigned the passage in its present form to the biographical material or to a non-Jeremianic source.[73] Duhm considered all of 27:12-22 and most of 27:1-11 to be the work of a later supplementor,[74] and regarded the passage as a whole as a later parallel to Jeremiah 28 (in the same way that Jer 7:1ff. corresponds to Jeremiah 26). Mowinckel,

---

[73]Duhm, *Das Buch Jeremia*, pp. 216ff.; Volz, *Der Prophet Jeremia* (Leipzig: A. Deichert, 1922), pp. 255ff.; Volz assigns it to an editor; Hyatt, *Jeremiah*, pp. 1009ff.; cf., however, Weiser, *Das Buch des Propheten Jeremia* (Göttingen: Vandenhoeck and Ruprecht, 1955), who includes the chapter in materials ascribed to Baruch, p. 245.

[74]Duhm, *Das Buch Jeremia*, pp. 216ff.

followed by many subsequent scholars, ascribed 27:1ff. to the Deuteronomistic C stratum.[75] He showed that the passage reflects many characteristic features of this source, such as a verbose and monotonous prose
style and the customary C diction; he noted also that vv. 5f. follow Jer
32:27f. (C) in form and content. Mowinckel found the conception of the
prophet in vs. 18 to be that of the C source; "the prophet is not a truth
teller but rather an intercessor and mediator between God and men, a
representative of religion."[76] The prophetic speech's indifference to the
historical setting in which it was uttered he found to be typical of C as
well. Hyatt argued that Jeremiah 27 is a Deuteronomistic revision of an
account which originally belonged to Baruch's memoirs,[77] and detected
Deuteronomistic diction especially in vv. 5, 8, 13. The editor of the
passage is responsible for the repetitious style and the "careless inter-
change of first and third persons."[78] According to Thiel's analysis, the
Deuteronomistic redactor of the book expanded an originally autobiographical report which is preserved in vv. 2-4, 11.[79] This judgment is
based on the presence of Deuteronomistic diction and the character of the
pericope with its concern for the problem of false prophecy (in vv. 9f., 14,
16f.) and the status of the temple implements (in vv. 16ff.; cf. 28:2).

The majority of these characteristic C features are *not* represented in
C'. Nine of the fifteen instances of the diction we have indexed are peculiar to the expanded text; only six are present in the common text (C'),
and these are all Type IV indices (phrases unattested in Deuteronomy and
Dtr). In this case few of the C features could have been integral to the
passage or (alternatively) introduced to it in the exilic period. They derive
for the most part from subsequent expansions and thus belong to a later
stage of the tradition.

29:1-32

That the MT is heavily expanded is evident from its tendency to fill out
personal names (vv. 3, 21 [four times], 32), add divine epithets (vv. 4, 8,
21), interpolate other passages (cf. vs. 1 with 24:1; cf. 14 with 16:15 and
32:37; cf. vs. 21 with 29:9; cf. vs. 32 with Deut 13:6), extend serial clauses

---

[75]Mowinckel, *Komposition,* p. 42.

[76]Ibid.

[77]Hyatt, "Deuteronomic Edition," p. 86; *Jeremiah,* pp. 1009ff.

[78]Hyatt, "Deuteronomic Edition," p. 86.

[79]Thiel, *Die deuteronomistische Redaktion,* 26-45, pp. 5ff.

(vv. 2, 6, 25), and supply ancillary formulae (vv. 9, 11, 14). Altogether the MT is 37 percent (or 192 words) longer than the OG *Vorlage*. While most of the MT plusses do not introduce new subject matter, at least two variants do so (vv. 14, 16-20). Verse 14 supplements the promise of an eventual return from exile in Babylon (vv. 10ff.) with a salvific prediction to restore and gather the *golah* "from all the nations and all the places" where Yahweh had scattered them. The lengthy MT plus in vv. 16-20 (ca. 100 words) apparently serves as an additional salvation oracle to those in exile and as a pronouncement of judgment upon Zedekiah and those with him in Jerusalem.[80]

(1) ואלה דברי הספר אשר שלח ירמיה הנביא מירושלם
אל-יתר זקני הגולה ואל-הכהנים ואל-הנביאים[1] ואל-
כל-העם אשר הגלה נבוכדנאצר מירושלם בבלה: (2)
אחרי צאת יכניה-המלך והגבירה והסריסים שרי יהודה
וירושלם והחרש והמסגר מירושלם: (3) ביד אלעשה בן-
שפן וגמריה בן-חלקיה אשר שלח צדקיה מלך-יהודה אל-
נבוכדנאצר מלך בבל בבלה לאמר: (4) כה אמר יהוה
צבאות אלהי ישראל לכל[X]-הגולה אשר-הגליתי מירושלם

---

[80]At least vv. 16-20 are commonly regarded as text peculiar to the MT, and therefore as secondary expansion. Ziegler's critical edition of the Greek text does not reckon these verses to the OG; it is then a reasonable inference that they were not present in the translator's *Vorlage*. The MT itself seems to support this judgment, for the verses are obviously out of place, disrupting the continuity between vv. 15 and 21. Some find additional support in the emphatically Deuteronomistic diction of the passage, but it would be begging the question if we took this into consideration ourselves since that is the very issue we are studying. The fact that vv. 15 and 20 end with identical words in Hebrew (*bblh*) complicates the issue, however. The possibility that the OG *Vorlage* may have been haplographic, or that haplography may have occurred subsequently in the course of the transmission of the OG, cannot be ruled out altogether; in that case, the disordered sequence of the MT would have to be accounted for separately. The matter is not easily resolved, but for the purposes of our analysis we will abide by the judgment of Ziegler and others and reckon vv. 16-20 to C+ (text peculiar to the MT) rather than to C' (the text common to the OG and the MT).

[1]OG adds *epistolēn eis Babulōna tē̜ apoikią̄*.
[2]OG reads *kai pantos eleutherou*.

בבלה: (5) בנו בתים ושבו ונטעו גנות ואכלו את-

פרין: (6) קחו נשים והולידו בנים ובנות וקחו לבניכם

נשים ואת-בנותיכם תנו לאנשים ותלדנה בנים ובנות ורבו-

שם ואל-תמעטו: (7) ודרשו את-שלום העיר[3] אשר הגליתי

אתכם שמה והתפללו בעדה אל-יהוה כי בשלומה יהיה[X]

לכם שלום: (8) כי כה אמר יהוה צבאות אלהי ישראל

אל-ישיאו לכם נביאיכם[4] אשר-בקרבכם[5] וקסמיכם ואל-

תשמעו אל-חלמתיכם אשר אתם מחלמים: (9) כי בשקר[X]

הם נבאים לכם בשמי לא[X] שלחתים נאם יהוה: (10) כי-

כה אמר יהוה כי לפי מלאת לבבל שבעים שנה אפקד

אתכם והקמתי עליכם את-דברי הטוב להשיב אתכם[X] אל-

המקום הזה: (11) כי אנכי [6]ידעתי את-המחשבת אשר אנכי[6]

חשב[X] עליכם נאם יהוה מחשבות שלום ולא לרעה לתת לכם

אחרית[X] ותקוה: (12) וקראתם אתי והלכתם והתפללתם

אלי ושמעתי אליכם: (13) ובקשתם אתי ומצאתם כי תדרשני

בכל-לבבכם: (14) ונמצאתי[7] לכם נאם-יהוה ושבתי את-

שביתכם וקבצתי אתכם מכל-הגוים ומכל-המקומות אשר

הדחתי אתכם שם נאם-יהוה והשבתי אתכם אל-המקום אשר-

הגליתי אתכם משם: (15) כי אמרתם הקים לנו יהוה

נבאים בבלה: (16) כי-כה אמר יהוה אל-המלך היושב בעיר

הזאת אחיכם אשר לא-יצאו אתכם בגולה: (17) כה אמר יהוה

צבאות הנני משלח בם את-החרב את-הרעב ואת-הדבר ונתתי

אותם כתאנים השערים אשר לא-תאכלנה מרע: (18) ורדפתי

אחריהם בחרב ברעב ובכדבר ונתתים לזועה לכל ממלכות

הארץ לאלה ולשמה ולשרקה ולחרפה בכל-הגוים אשר הדחתים

שם: (19) תחת אשר-לא-שמעו אל-דברי נאם-יהוה אשר

שלחתי אליהם את-עבדי הנבאים השכם ושלח ולא שמעתם

נאם יהוה: (20) ואתם שמעו דבר-יהוה כל-הגולה אשר-

שלחתי מירושלם בבלה: (21) כה-אמר יהוה צבאות אלהי

ישראל אל-אחאב בן-קוליה ואל-צדקיהו בן-מעשיה הנבאים

לכם בשמי שקר הנני נתן אתם ביד נבוכדראצר מלך-בבל

והכם לעיניכם: (22) ולקח מהם קללה לכל[X] גלות יהודה

אשר[X] בבבל לאמר ישמך יהוה כצדקיהו וכאחב אשר-קלם

---

[3]OG reads *tēs gēs*.

[4]OG reads *pseudoprophētai* without the suffix.

[5]OG adds *mē anapeithetōsan humas*.

[6]May be omitted in OG by homoeoteleuton.

[7]OG reads *kai epiphanoumai*.

מלך־בבל באש: (23) יען אשר עשו נבלה בישראל וינאפו
את־נשי רעיהם וידברו^X דבר^X בשמי שקר אשר לוא
צויתם ואנכי היודע ועד נאם יהוה: (24) ואל־שמעיהו
הנחלמי תאמר לאמר: (25) כה אמר יהוה צבאות אלהי
ישראל לאמר ^{8}יען אשר אתה שלחת בשמכה^8 ספרים אל־כל־
העם אשר בירושלם ואל־צפניה בן־מעשיה הכהן ואל כל־
הכהנים לאמר: (26) יהוה נתנך כהן תחת יהוידע הכהן
להיות פקדים^X בת^X יהוה לכל־איש משגע ומתנבא^9 ונתתה
אתו אל־המהפכת ואל־הצינק: (27) ועתה למה לא נערת^X
בירמיהו הענתתי^X המתנבא לכם: (28) כי על־כן שלח
אלינו בבל לאמר ארכה היא בנו בתים ושבו ונטעו גנות
ואכלו את־פריהם: (29) ויקרא צפניה הכהן את־הספר הזה
באזני ירמיהו הנביא: (30) ויהי דבר־יהוה אל־ירמיהו
לאמר: (31) שלח על^X־כל־הגולה לאמר כה אמר יהוה אל־
שמעיה הנחלמי יען אשר נבא לכם שמעיה ואני לא שלחתיו
ויבטח אתכם על־שקר: (32) לכן כה־אמר יהוה הנני פקד
על־שמעיה הנחלמי ועל־זרעו ^{10}לא־יהיה לו איש יושב
בתוך־העם הזה ולא־יראה בטוב^{10} אשר־אני עשה־לעמי^X
נאם־יהוה כי־סרה דבר על־יהוה:

		C'	C		C'	C
Type I:	5. (vs. 19)	–	X	15. (vs. 10)	X	X
	11. (vs. 18)	–	X	17. (vs. 13)	X	X
Type II:	39. (vs. 18)	–	X			
Type III:	51. (vs. 14)	–	X	52. (vs. 18)	–	X
	52. (vs. 14)	–	X	56. (vs. 18)	–	X
Type IV:	68. (vs. 4)	–	Xc	70. (vs. 19)	–	X
	68. (vs. 8)	–	Xc	75. (vs. 9)	X	X
	68. (vs. 21)	–	Xc	75. (vs. 21)	–	X
	68. (vs. 25)	–	X	76. (vs. 32)	X	X
	69. (vs. 17)	–	X	80. (vs. 8)	–	Xc
	69. (vs. 18)	–	X	87. (vs. 31)	X	X

[8]OG reads *ouk apesteila se tǭ onomati mou.*

[9]OG adds *panti anthrōpǭ.*

[10]OG reads *kai ouk estai autǭ anthrōpos en mesǭ humōn tou idein ta agatha.*

Summary Tabulation of Instances

	I	II	III	IV	totals
C':	2	-	-	3	5
C+:	2	1	4	9	16
C:	4	1	4	12	21

Although Rudolph and Weiser attribute Jeremiah 29 to Baruch, Mowinckel, Hyatt, Nicholson, *et al.*[81] ascribe the chapter wholly or in part to a Deuteronomistic hand on the basis of its diction, style, and ideas. In spite of the fact that it does not have the characteristic introductory formula, Mowinckel included 29:1-23 in his Deuteronomistic C stratum, although primarily by process of elimination.[82] He found interpolations, glosses and unauthentic additions to be scattered indiscriminately throughout the composition. The remainder of the chapter (vv. 24ff.) he regarded as parallel B material, an association he found to be typical of C passages which lacked the introductory sentence. According to Hyatt, chap. 29 in its present form is a partial revision of Jeremiah's letter to the exiles in Babylon (which is preserved intact in vv. 4-9)—a piece which was originally in Baruch's memoirs.[83] Verses 10-20 show much evidence of Deuteronomic diction and ideas and are thus most probably from the Deuteronomic editor of the book. Nicholson has assigned the greater part of chap. 29 to Deuteronomistic traditionists who were concerned with the problem of false prophecy (cf. chaps. 27 and 28) and employed Deuteronomistic and Deuteronomic ideas in order to come to terms with this problem. For example, the Deuteronomic penalty of death demanded for false prophets is pronounced upon Shemaiah for speaking rebellion against Yahweh (vv. 29ff., cf. Deut 13:2-6).[84] The verbose nature of the serial clauses and the reproduction of the Dtr *Prophetenaussage* in vv. 17-19 are also indicative of the passage's association with Deuteronomistic tradition.

While 29:1ff. manifests several significant points of contact with

---

[81]See Nicholson, *Preaching,* pp. 97ff.; Thiel, *Die deuteronomistische Redaktion,* 26-45, pp. 11ff.

[82]Mowinckel, *Komposition,* pp. 40-42.

[83]Hyatt, "Deuteronomic Edition," pp. 86f.; *Jeremiah,* p. 1016.

[84]Nicholson, *Preaching,* pp. 97ff.; cf. also vv. 8f. with Deut 18:10-14; vv. 10f. with Jer 25:11f.; vv. 13f. with Deut 4:29, 30:1-5; vs. 23 with Deut 18:20; vv. 30-32 with Deut 8:6, 13:2-6.

Deuteronomistic tradition, our analysis shows that only 23 percent of the
instances of C diction which we have identified in this chapter (five of the
twenty-one) are actually attested in Dtr. An even smaller percentage is
attested in the Deuteronomic corpus (19 percent or four of twenty-one).
The majority are peculiar to the Jeremianic prose sermons or appear
elsewhere in the biblical materials (57 percent or twelve of twenty-one).
Thus as a whole the chapter seems to employ the stock phraseology of the
C corpus as well as occasional ideas and language from Deuteronomistic
tradition.

Even this characterization of 29:1ff. is applicable only to the C text
(which includes the C+ expansions) and not the common text (C') which is
markedly shorter. Only five of the twenty-one instances of C diction are
represented in C'. The text's repetitive style, especially evident in the
serial clauses, and the Deuteronomistic theme of prophetic warning,
Israel's rejection, and Yahweh's subsequent judgment (i.e., the *Prophetenaussage*) are represented fully only in C/C+. Consequently, the current
understandings of the characteristic C features by proponents of the
redaction hypothesis and their critics alike require reconsideration for Jer
29:1ff. For the most part these features derive from subsequent expansions.

32:1-44

Here, as in most prose sermons in the book of Jeremiah, the MT has a
longer text than the OG *Vorlage*. The difference is seventy-three words,
which means that 10 percent of the MT is C+ expansion. While the two
witnesses differ little with respect to subject matter and arrangement,
the MT again reflects a more developed textual tradition. The majority of
MT plusses are relatively small and do not introduce significant changes.
Instead, they frequently stress details that are already present in C' or
undertake to clarify them. One finds names and clichés which have been
expanded to their full form (e.g., vv. 28, 44), additional titles (e.g., vv. 1,
2, 3, 4) and divine epithets (e.g., vv. 14, 15, 18, 25), and (explanatory)
glosses (vv. 5b, 11, 12, 14, passim), all of which are characteristic of the
MT of Jeremiah as a whole. There are also several content (or qualitative)
variants. In most cases these involve pronominal suffixes which have been
made explicit (vv. 6, 26), apparent discrepancies in person (vv. 6, 26), and
differences in the rendering of certain words (e.g., vv. 8, 17, 36).

(1) הדבר אשר-היה אל-ירמיהו מאת יהוה בשנת העשרית
לצדקיהו מלך יהודה היא השנה שמנה-עשרה שנה לנבוכדראצר[1]:
(2) אז[X] חיל מלך בבל צרים על-ירושלם וירמיהו הנביא
היה[X] כלוא בחצר המטרה אשר בית-מלך יהודה: (3) אשר כלאו
צדקיהו מלך-יהודה לאמר מדוע אתה נבא לאמר כה אמר
יהוה הנני נתן את-העיר הזאת ביד מלך-בבל ולכדה:
(4) וצדקיהו מלך יהודה לא ימלט מיד הכשדים כי
הנתן ינתן ביד מלך-בבל ודבר-פיו עם-פיו ועיניו
את-עיניו תראינה: (5) ובבל יולך את-צדקיהו ושם
יהיה[X] עד-פקדי אתו נאם-יהוה כי תלחמו את-הכשדים
לא תצליחו: (6) ויאמר ירמיהו [2]היה דבר-יהוה אלי[2]
לאמר: (7) הנה חנמאל בן-שלם דדך בא אליך לאמר קנה
לך את-שדי אשר בענתות כי לך משפט הגאלה לקנות:
(8) ויבא אלי חנמאל בן[X]-דדי כדבר יהוה אל-חצר
המטרה ויאמר אלי קנה נא[X] את-שדי אשר [3]בענתות אשר
בארץ בנימין[3] כי-לך משפט הירשה ולך הגאלה[X] קנה-לך
ואדע כי דבר-יהוה הוא: (9) ואקנה את-השדה מאת[X]
חנמאל בן-דדי אשר בענתות ואשקלה-לו את-הכסף שבעה
שקלים ועשרה הכסף: (10) ואכתב בספר ואחתם ואעד
עדים ואשקל הכסף במאזנים: (11) ואקח את-ספר המקנה
את-החתום המצוה והחקים ואת-הגלוי: (12) [4]ואתן את-
הספר המקנה[X] אל-ברוך בן-נריה בן-מחסיה לעיני
חנמאל [X]דדי ולעיני העדים[X] הכתבים בספר המקנה לעיני
כל-היהודים הישבים בחצר המטרה: (13) ואצוה את-
ברוך לעיניהם לאמר: (14) כה-אמר יהוה צבאות אלהים
ישראל לקוח את-הספרים האלה את ספר המקנה הזה
ואת החתום ואת ספר הגלוי הזה ונתתם[X] בכלי-חרש
למען יעמדו[X] ימים רבים: (15) כי כה אמר יהוה
צבאות אלהי ישראל[X] עוד יקנו בתים[X] ושדות[X] וכרמים
בארץ הזאת: (16) ואתפלל אל-יהוה אחרי תתי את-
ספר המקנה אל-ברוך בן-נריה לאמר: (17) אהה אדני
יהוה הנה[X] אתה עשית את-השמים ואת-הארץ בכחך הגדול
ובזרעך הנטויה לא-יפלא[X] ממך כל-דבר: (18) עשה
חסד לאלפים ומשלם עון אבות אל-חיק בניהם אחריהם
האל הגדול הגבור יהוה צבאות שמו: (19) גדל העצה

---

[1]OG adds *basilei Babulōnos*.
[2]OG reads *kai logos kuriou egenēthē pros Ieremian.*
[3]OG has a different order.
[4]OG reads *kai edōka auto . . . .*

ורב העליליה ^{5}אשר-עיניך פקחות על^X-כל-דרכי בני
אדם לתת לאיש כדרכיו^X וכפרי מעלליו: (20) אשר-
שמת אתות ומפתים בארץ-מצרים עד-היום הזה ובישראל
ובאדם ותעשה-לך שם כיום הזה: (21) ותצא את-עמך
את-ישראל מארץ מצרים באתות ובמופתים וביד חזקה
ובאזרוע נטויה ובמורא גדול: (22) ותתן להם את-
הארץ הזאת אשר-נשבעת לאבותם לתת להם ארץ זבת
חלב ודבש: (23) ויבאו וירשו אתה ולא-שמעו בקולך
ובתרותך לא-הלכו את כל-אשר צויתה להם לעשות לא
עשו ותקרא אתם את כל-הרעה^X הזאת^X: (24) הנה
הסללות^X באו העיר ללכדה והעיר נתנה ביד הכשדים
הנלחמים עליה מפני החרב והרעב והדבר ואשר^X דברת
היה והנך ראה (25) ואתה אמרת אלי אדני יהוה קנה-
לך השדה בכסף^6 והעד^X עדים והעיר נתנה ביד הכשדים:
(26) ^{7}ויהי דבר-יהוה אל-ירמיהו^7 לאמר: (27) הנה^X אני
יהוה אלהי כל-בשר הממני יפלא^X כל-דבר: (28) לכן כה
אמר יהוה הנני נתן^X את-העיר הזאת ביד הכשדים וביד
נבוכדראצר מלך-בבל ולכדה: (29) ובאו הכשדים הנלחמים
על-העיר הזאת והציתו את-העיר הזאת באש ושרפוה^X ואת^X
הבתים אשר קטרו על-גגותיהם לבעל והסכו נסכים לאלהים
אחרים למען הכעסני: (30) כי-היו בני-ישראל ובני
יהודה אך עשים הרע בעיני מנעריהם כי בני-ישראל אך
מכעסים אתי במעשה ידיהם נאם-יהוה: (31) כי על-אפי
ועל-חמתי היתה לי העיר הזאת למן^X-היום אשר בנו
אותה ועל היום הזה להסירה מעל פני: (32) על כל-רעת
בני-ישראל ובני יהודה אשר עשו להכעסני המה מלכיהם
שריהם כהניהם ונביאיהם ואיש^X יהודה וישבי ירושלם:
(33) ויפנו אלי ערף ולא פנים ולמד^X אתם השכם ולמד
ואינם שמעים^X לקחת מוסר: (34) וישימו שקוציהם בבית
אשר-נקרא-שמי עליו לטמאו^X: (35) ויבנו את-במות הבעל
אשר בגיא בן-הנם להעביר את-בניהם ואת-בנותיהם ומלך
אשר לא-צויתים ולא עלתה על-לבי לעשות התועבה הזאת
למען החטי את-יהודה: (36) ועתה לכן כה-אמר יהוה
אלהי ישראל אל-העיר הזאת אשר אתם אמרים נתנה^X ביד
מלך-בבל בחרב וברעב ובדבר^8: (37) הנני מקבצם מכל-

---

^{5}OG adds *ho theos ho megas ho pantokratōr ho megalōnumos kurios.*
^{6}OG adds *kai egrapsa biblion kai esphragisamēn.*
^{7}OG reads *kai egeneto logos kurios pros me.*
^{8}OG reads *kai en apostolē.*

הארצות^X אשר הדחתים שם באפי ובחמתי ובקצף גדול
והשבתים אל־המקום הזה והשבתים לבטח^X: (38) והיו לי
לעם ואני אהיה להם לאלהים: (39) ונתתי להם ⁹לב אחד
ודרך אחד⁹ ליראה אותי כל־הימים לטוב להם ולבניהם
אחריהם: (40) וכרתי להם ברית עולם אשר לא־אשוב^X
מאחריהם להיטיבי אותם ואת־יראתי אתן בלבבם לבלתי
סור מעלי: (41) ¹⁰וששתי עליהם ¹⁰ להטיב אותם ונטעתים
בארץ הזאת באמת בכל־לבי ובכל־נפשי^X: (42) כי־כה אמר
יהוה כאשר הבאתי אל^X־העם הזה את כל־הרעה^X הגדולה
הזאת כן אנכי מביא עליהם את־כל־הטובה^X אשר אנכי^X
דבר^X עליהם: (43) ונקנה^X השדה^X בארץ הזאת אשר אתם
אמרים שממה היא מאין אדם ובהמה נתנה ביד הכשדים:
(44) שדות^X בכסף יקנו^X וכתוב בספר וחתום והעד עדים
בארץ בנימן ובסביבי ירושלם ובערי יהודה ובערי ההר
ובערי השפלה ובערי^X הנגב כי־אשיב את־שבותם נאם יהיה:

		C'	C		C'	C
Type I:	1. (vs. 23)	X	X	19. (vs. 34)	X	X
	7. (vs. 29)	X	X	20. (vs. 35)	X	X
	7. (vs. 32)	X	X	22. (vs. 41)	X	X
	8. (vs. 30)	-	X	25. (vs. 39)	X	X
	9. (vs. 30)	X	X	26. (vs. 35)	X	X
	14. (vs. 20)	X	X	27. (vs. 40)	X	X
	16. (vs. 22)	X	X	34. (vs. 31)	X	X
	18. (vs. 21)	X	X	35. (vs. 23)	X	X
				37. (vs. 21)	X	X
Type II:	38. (vs. 29)	X	X	44. (vs. 38)	X	X
	40. (vs. 34)	X	X	45. (vs. 23)	X	X
	41. (vs. 32)	X	X	50. (vs. 17)	X	X
Type III:	51. (vs. 44)	X	X	57. (vs. 37)	X	X
	52. (vs. 37)	X	X	61. (vs. 41)	-	Xc
Type IV:	68. (vs. 14)	-	Xc	71. (vs. 1)	X	X
	68. (vs. 15)	-	Xc	73. (vs. 43)	X	X
	69. (vs. 24)	-	Xc	79. (vs. 33)	X	X
	69. (vs. 36)	-	Xc	80. (vs. 32)	X	X
	70. (vs. 33)	X	X	84. (vs. 35)	X	X
				88. (vs. 32)	X	X

---

[9] OG has a different order.
[10] OG reads *kai episkepsomai autous.*

Summary Tabulation of Instances

	I	II	III	IV	totals
C':	16	6	3	7	32
C+:	1	-	1	4	6
C:	17	6	4	11	38

Jer 32 has generally been regarded as C material on the grounds that Deuteronomistic diction and ideology pervade it; but analyses have differed considerably in detail. Mowinckel assigned vv. 1f. 6-16, 24-44 to his Deuteronomistic C source. He excluded vv. 17-23 (in spite of their occasional Deuteronomistic diction) because these verses disrupt the continuity between vv. 6-16 and vv. 24-44: if the prophet had already affirmed that "nothing is too wonderful for Yahweh" (in vv. 17-23), the subsequent question and divine reply (vv. 26ff.) would have been superfluous.[85] He judged that vv. 17-23 had been added later in the redaction of the passage. In vv. 24ff., he identified several characteristic motifs of his Deuteronomistic source, including Judah's uninterrupted sins depicted in cultic terms (vv. 29, 32f.) and the ensuing judgment of Yahweh for such idolatrous acts (vs. 36). Against Mowinckel, Hyatt assigned the major part of the chapter to a Deuteronomistic hand, including vv. 17-23. (Verses 1 and 6-15, however, he ascribed to Baruch, and vv. 2-5 to a later editor). In his view the whole editorial section, vv. 16-44, provides "almost a summary of the theology and conception of Hebrew history held by the Deuteronomists."[86] Leslie found the "ecclesiastical prayer" in vv. 17-23 and the long interpolation in vv. 29b-41 to be the work of an exilic Deuteronomistic editor.[87] The latter section in particular "abounds in phrases and concepts such as characterize the Deuteronomistic editor of the book, as a comparison of vvs. 29b-41 with 7:12-31 readily shows."[88] Herrmann considered vv. 36-44, 15 to be Deuteronomistic salvation oracles,[89] and argued that the salvific ideas which emerge in these verses are only fully understood and appreciated against the background of Deuteronomistic tradition. Verses 36-44 employ entirely conventional language to express Yahweh's future plan of salvation for the exiles. The people of God have

---

[85]Mowinckel, *Komposition*, p. 31.

[86]Hyatt, "Deuteronomic Edition," p. 87.

[87]Leslie, *Jeremiah*, pp. 328f.

[88]Ibid., p. 328.

[89]Herrmann, *Heilserwartungen*, pp. 187f.

been dispersed to distant lands as a result of Yahweh's indignation but will be brought back to Jerusalem ("this place") through his kindness (cf. 27:10; 29:14; 24:6, 9). When the *golah* will have returned to Jerusalem, Yahweh will reaffirm his covenant commitment with them to be "their God" (vs. 38). He will, moreover, place the "fear of God" in their heart (= implanting the Torah in the hearts of his people, 31:33; cf. Deut 6:4ff.) and will establish an "everlasting covenant" for their permanent well-being (vv. 39f.; cf. 31:31ff.). Yahweh will then treat his restored people with wholehearted affection and benevolence. Verse 41 is a unique reversal of a Deuteronomic idiom which was originally employed with respect to the people's attitude towards the deity (Deut 6:4).

Apart from the customary introductory sentence (vs. 1) and two prophetic formulae (vv. 14, 15), all of the characteristic C diction appears in Jeremiah's prayer (vv. 16-25) and Yahweh's answer (vv. 26-44). For the most part the diction we have indexed is represented fully in C' (thirty-two of thirty-eight instances). The few instances which C+ expansions have added—often by completing phrases already present in C'—are largely of the type not attested in Dtr or Deuteronomy (our Type IV, four of six instances). In this chapter the explicit Deuteronomistic diction (our Types I and II) is more characteristic of C' (twenty-two of thirty-two instances) than of C+.

33:1-26

Textual variants in vv. 1-13 are relatively few, and the majority of those which do occur conform to the general tendency. The MT inflates prophetic formulae (vv. 4, 11) and develops certain readings from parallel and/or related contexts (e.g., vs. 10 ומין יושב ומאין perhaps from a related cliché found in Jer 26:9; 34:22; vs. 12 מאין אדם ועד בהמה probably from a similar expression in vs. 10).[90] Verses 14-26 are unattested in the OG. We concur with Janzen that these verses were most probably "added to the proto-M tradition after the divergence of the two text traditions."[91]

(1) ויהי דבר־יהוה אל־ירמיהו שנית והוא עודנו
עצור בחצר המטרה לאמר: (2) כה־אמר יהוה ¹עשה

---

[90] Janzen, *Studies,* pp. 49f., 66.
[91] Ibid., p. 123.

יהוה[1] יוצר[X] אותה להכינה יהוה שמו: (3) קרא אלי
ואענך ואגידה לך גדלות ובצרות[X] לא ידעתם: (4) כי
כה אמר יהוה אלהי ישראל על-בתי העיר הזאת ועל-
בתי מלכי[X] יהודה הנתצים אל-הסללות ואל-החרב[X]:
(5) באים להלחם את[X]-הכשדים ולמלאם[X] את-פגרי האדם
אשר-הכיתי באפי ובחמתי ואשר[X] הסתרתי פני [2]מהעיר
הזאת[2] על כל-רעתם: (6) הנני מעלה-לה ארכה ומרפא
[3]ורפאתים וגליתי להם[3] עתרת[X] שלום ואמת: (7)
והשבתי את-שבות יהודה ואת שבות ישראל ובנתים
כבראשנה: (8) וטהרתים מכל-עונם אשר חטאו-לי
וסלחתי לכל-עונותיהם אשר חטאו-לי ואשר[X] פשעו
בי: (9) והיתה לי לשם ששון לתהלה ולתפארת לכל
גויי הארץ אשר ישמעו את-כל-הטובה אשר אנכי
עשה אתם ופחדו ורגזו על כל-הטובה ועל כל-השלום
אשר אנכי עשה לה[X]: (10) כה אמר יהוה עוד ישמע
במקום-הזה אשר אתם אמרים חרב הוא מאין <u>אדם ומאין</u>
<u>בהמה בעיר יהודה ובחצות ירושלם הנשמות מאין אדם</u>
<u>ומאין יושב ומאין בהמה</u>: (11) <u>קול ששון וקול שמחה</u>
<u>קול חתן וקול כלה קול</u> אמרים הודו את-יהוה צבאות
כי-טוב יהוה כי-לעולם חסדו מבאים תודה בית יהוה
כי-<u>אשיב את-שבות-הארץ כבראשנה אמר יהוה</u>: (12) כה-
אמר יהוה צבאות עוד יהיה במקום הזה החרב מאין-
<u>אדם ועד-בהמה</u> ובכל-<u>עריו</u> נוה רעים מרבצים צאן: (13)
בערי ההר בערי[X] השפלה ובערי הנגב ובארץ בנימן
ובסביבי ירושלם ובערי יהודה עד תעברנה הצאן על-
ידי אמר יהוה: (14) <u>הנה ימים באים נאם-יהוה והקמתי</u>
<u>את-הדבר הטוב אשר דברתי אל-בית ישראל ועל-בית יהודה</u>:
(15) בימים ההם ובעת ההוא אצמיח לדוד צמח צדקה ועשה
משפט וצדקה בארץ: (16) בימים ההם תושע יהודה וירושלם
תשכון לבטח וזה אשר-יקרא-לה יהוה צדקנו: (17) כי-כה
אמר יהוה לא-יכרת לדוד איש ישב על-כסא בית-ישראל:
(18) ולכהנים הלוים לא-יכרת איש מלפני מעלה עולה
ומקטיר מנחה ועשה זבח כל-הימים: (19) ויהי דבר-יהוה
אל-ירמיהו לאמור: (20) כה אמר יהוה אם-תפרו את-בריתי
היום ואת-בריתי הלילה ולבלתי היות יומם-ולילה בעתם:

---

[1]OG reads *poiōn gēn kai*.

[2]OG reads *ap' autōn*.

[3]OG reads *kai poiēsō*.

(21) גם-בריתי תפר את-דוד עבדי מהיות-לו בן מלך
על-כסאו ואת-הלוים הכהנים משרתי: (22) אשר לא-יספר
צבא השמים ולא ימד חול הים כן ארבה את-זרע דוד
עבדי ואת-הלוים משרתי אתי: (23) ויהי דבר-יהוה אל-
ירמיהו לאמר: (24) הלוא ראית מה-העם הזה דברו
לאמר שתי המשפחות אשר <u>בחר יהוה</u> בהם וימאסם ואת-עמי
ינאצון מהיות עוד גוי לפניהם: (25) כה אמר יהוה אם-לא
בריתי יומם ולילה חקום שמים וארץ לא-שמתי: (26) גם-זרע
יעקוב ודוד עבדי אמאס מקחת מזרעו משלים אל-זרע אברהם
ישחק ויעקב כי-<u>אשוב את-שבותם</u> ורחמתים:

		C'	C		C'	C
Type I:	15. (vs. 14)	–	X	31. (vs. 24)	–	X
				32. (vs. 17)	–	X
Type II:	43. (vs. 14)	–	X			
Type III:	51. (vs. 7)	X	X	51. (vs. 11)	X	X
				51. (vs. 26)	–	X
Type IV:	73. (vs. 10)	X	X	73. (vs. 12)	–	X
	73. (vs. 10)	X	X	74. (vs. 10)	X	X
				78. (vs. 11)	X	X

Summary Tabulation of Instances

	I	II	III	IV	totals
C':	–	–	2	4	6
C+:	3	1	1	1	6
C:	3	1	3	5	12

The two major blocks of material in this chapter (vv. 1-13 and 14-26)
exhibit relatively few characteristic C features. Hyatt and Nicholson have
identified a few points of contact between the first complex of sayings
and the Deuteronomistic and Jeremianic prose traditions.[92] While admit-
ting that the evidence is not strong, Hyatt detects D diction in vv. 9, 11

---

[92]Hyatt, "Deuteronomic Edition," p. 87; Nicholson, *Preaching,* pp. 85,
133.

and suggests that this section may be a Deuteronomistic revision of "some incident which is now obscurely preserved in vv. 4-5, where the text is difficult to understand."[93] Nicholson notes that the promise in vv. 6ff., 10f., and 12f., which embodies expectations for Israel's future, parallels other passages in the Jeremianic prose tradition.[94] According to our own list of linguistic indices, characteristic C diction appears in vv. 7, 10 and 11. It could also be said that the judgment oracle in v. 5 and the salvation oracle in vv. 6ff. lack the creative images and ideas which are typical of the authentic Jeremianic sayings and instead employ stereotyped and monotonous conventional language which is closer to Dtr. The remaining vv. 14-26 most critics—with the notable exception of Nicholson—have viewed as a very late (post-exilic) non-Jeremianic interpolation, on the grounds that they are absent from the LXX and seem to reflect theological ideas representative of fifth or fourth century Judaism. While conceding that the passage is indicative of a "late stage in the development of the Jeremianic prose tradition," Nicholson has suggested that the usual post-exilic date is not entirely warranted. He reasons that the block of material should be ascribed to a late stage in the exilic period, since it employs Dtr diction (vv. 14,17) and the Dtr prophecy-fulfillment schema (v. 14)—"one of the most characteristic features of the Deuteronomistic theology."[95]

In vv. 1-13, six of the seven instances of C diction we have indexed are represented fully in C'. None of the seven is attested in Dtr, however, and only two are attested in Deuteronomy, so the links with Deuteronomistic diction are indirect at best. On the other hand, in vv. 14-26 (which is wholly a C+ expansion) four of the five instances are attested in Dtr and the fifth in Deuteronomy. This is one of the few chapters in which the C+ expansions are more Deuteronomistic than the common text, although it must be added that instances of C diction are relatively few in either case.

34:1-22

The majority of the variants are quantitative. The MT exhibits a relatively high number of plusses; it is 19 percent, or seventy-six words, longer than the reconstructed OG *Vorlage.* The expansions for the most

---

[93]Hyatt, "Deuteronomic Edition," p. 87.

[94]Nicholson, *Preaching,* p. 133.

[95]Ibid., p. 90.

part conform to the kind of plusses found elsewhere in the C material. Many are taken from parallel or related contexts in the book of Jeremiah.[96] The vast majority do not introduce new subject matter or alter the text in significant ways. There are exceptions, however, and several of these should be noted. The MT seems to go out of its way to involve the people and officials of Jerusalem in vv. 8, 19, and 22 (where the MT has הזאת העיר), whereas the OG *Vorlage* speaks more generally of the people, Judah, or the land (cf. v. 22, where it reads הזאת הארץ). This is probably deliberate; the same tendency can be seen in 29:25, which goes out of its way to involve "all the people who are in Jerusalem" and "all the priests." The somewhat enigmatic content variant in vs. 18b, where the Greek τον μοσχον ον εποιησαν εργαζεσθαι αυτον differs radically from the Hebrew בתריו בין ויעברו לשנים כרתו אשר העגל, is another case in point. The MT reading seems to have been shaped by the covenant incident in Genesis 15 (the covenant with Abraham), even though there it was only Yahweh who passed symbolically through the pieces. The variant in the OG *Vorlage* seems to have Exodus 32 (the golden bull [ʿgl] incident) in mind instead. Both apparently intend to associate the covenant of Jeremiah 34 with the great covenants of the past, perhaps to make the seriousness of the offence all the more obvious and the threat of punishment even more terrible.

הדבר אשר־היה אל־ירמיהו מאת יהוה ונבוכדראצר[x] (1)
מלך־בבל וכל־חילו וכל־ממלכות ארץ ממשלת[x] ידו וכל־
העמים נלחמים על־ירושלם ועל־כל־עריה[1] לאמר: (2)
כה־אמר יהוה אלהי ישראל הלך ואמרת אל־צדקיהו מלך
יהודה ואמרת אליו כה אמר יהוה הנני נתן[x] את־העיר
הזאת ביד מלך־בבל[2] ושרפה באש: (3) ואתה לא המלט
מידו כי[x] תפש תתפש וביד תנתן ועיניך[3] את־עיני
מלך־בבל[3] תראינה ופיהו את־פיך ידבר ובכל תבוא:
(4) אך שמע דבר־יהוה צדקיהו מלך יהודה כה־אמר
יהוה עליך לא תמות בחרב: (5) בשלום תמות וכמשרפות[x]
אבותיך המלכים הראשנים אשר־היו לפניך כן ישרפו[x]־
לך והוי אדון יספדו־לך כי־דבר אני[x]־דברתי נאם־
יהוה: (6) וידבר ירמיהו הנביא אל־צדקיהו מלך יהודה

---

[96]Janzen, *Studies*, pp. 51f.

[1]OG reads *poleis Iouda*.
[2]OG adds *kai sullēmpsetai autēn*.
[3]OG reads *tou ophthalmous autou*.

את כל-הדברים האלה בירושלם: (7) וחיל מלך-בבל
נלחמים^X על-ירושלם ועל כל-ערי יהודה הנותרות
אל-לכיש ואל-עזקה כי הנה^X נשארו בערי יהודה ערי
מבצר: (8) <u>הדבר אשר-היה אל-ירמיהו מאת יהוה אחרי</u>
כרת המלך צדקיהו ברית את-כל-העם אשר בירושלם
לקרא להם^X דרור: (9) לשלח איש את-עבדו ואיש את-
שפחתו העברי והעבריה חפשים לבלתי <u>עבד-בם</u>^X ביהודי
אחיהו איש: (10) וישמעו^X כל-השרים וכל-העם אשר-
באו בברית לשלח איש את-עבדו ואיש את-שפחתו חפשים
לבלתי <u>עבד-בם</u> עוד וישמעו וישלחו: (11) וישובו
אחרי-כן וישבו את-העבדים ואת-השפחות אשר שלחו
חפשים ויכבישום לעבדים ולשפחות: (12) ויהי דבר-
יהוה אל-ירמיהו מאת יהוה לאמר: (13) כה-אמר יהוה
אלהי ישראל אנכי כרתי ברית את-אבותיכם ביום
<u>הוצאי אותם מארץ מצרים מבית עבדים</u> לאמר: (14)
מקץ שבע^4 שנים תשלחו^X איש^X את-אחיו העברי אשר-
ימכר לך ועבדך שש שנים ושלחתו חפשי מעמך ולא-שמעו
אבותיכם אלי ולא הטו את-אזנם: (15) ותשבו^X אתם^X
היום ותעשו את-הישר בעיני לקרא דרור איש לרעהו
ותכרתו^X ברית לפני בבית אשר-נקרא שמי עליו: (16)
ותשבו ותחללו את-שמי ותשבו^X איש את-עבדו ואיש
את-שפחתו אשר-שלחתם חפשים לנפשם ותכבשו אתם להיות
לכם לעבדים ולשפחות: (17) לכן כה-אמר יהוה אתם
לא-שמעתם אלי לקרא דרור איש לאחיו ואיש לרעהו הנני
קרא לכם דרור נאם-יהוה אל-<u>החרב אל^X-הדבר ואל-הרעב</u>
<u>ונתתי אתכם לזועה לכל ממלכות הארץ:</u> (18) ונתתי את-
האנשים העברים את-ברתי אשר לא-הקימו את-<u>דברי הברית</u>^X
אשר כרתו לפני העגל אשר ^5כרתו לשנים ויעברו בין
בתריו^5: (19) שרי יהודה ושרי ירושלם הסרסים הכהנים
וכל עם הארץ העברים בין בתרי העגל: (20) ונתתי אותם
ביד איביהם וביד <u>מבקשי נפשם והיתה נבלתם למאכל לעוף</u>
<u>השמים ולבהמת הארץ:</u> (21) ואת-צדקיהו מלך-יהודה ואת
שריו^X אתן ביד איביהם וביד <u>מבקשם נפשם</u> וביד חיל מלך
בבל העלים^X מעליכם: (22) הנני מצוה נאם-יהוה והשבתים
אל-העיר^6 הזאת ונלחמו עליה ולכדוה ושרפה באש ואת-
ערי יהודה אתן^X שממה^X מאין ישב:

---

[4]OG reads *hex etē*.

[5]OG reads *epoiēsan ergazesthai autǭ*.

[6]OG reads *eis tēn gēn tautēn*.

		C'	C		C'	C
Type I:	2. (vs. 13)	X	X	11. (vs. 1)	-	Xc
	9. (vs. 15)	X	X	11. (vs. 17)	X	X
Type II:	40. (vs. 15)	X	X	42. (vs. 18)	-	Xc
Type III:	53. (vs. 20)	X	X	56. (vs. 17)	X	X
				59. (vs. 13)	X	X
Type IV:	69. (vs. 17)	X	X	77. (vs. 20)	-	X
	71. (vs. 1)	X	X	77. (vs. 21)	-	X
	71. (vs. 8)	X	X	81. (vs. 9)	-	Xc
	72. (vs. 14)	X	X	81. (vs. 10)	-	X

Summary Tabulation of Instances

	I	II	III	IV	totals
C':	3	1	3	4	11
C+:	1	1	-	4	6
C:	4	2	3	8	17

Mowinckel assigned vv. 1-7 to his Deuteronomistic C source, primarily on the basis of the introductory formula (v. 1) and the customary prophecy of judgment.[97] He conceded, however, that this passage differs markedly from other C materials, in that it and 21:1-10 are the only oracles in this stratum which have a clear rhythm, a continuous *parallelismus membrorum,* and an unequivocal poetic sense. Against Mowinckel's assessment, the majority of commentators have ascribed 34:1-7 to the B material for some of the following reasons: the passage is a narrative account which supplies many circumstantial details (e.g., vv. 1, 6f.); Jeremiah is referred to only in the third person, that is, the text is basically biographical (*Er-Bericht*) and not autobiographical (*Ich-Bericht*); the passage contains a promise to Zedekiah which was not fulfilled.[98] In view of the fact that

[97]Mowinckel, *Komposition,* pp. 31,33.

[98]For example, Rudolph, *Jeremia,* pp. xiv, 187ff.; Leslie, *Jeremiah,* pp. 230f.; Hyatt, "Deuteronomic Edition," p. 87; *Jeremiah,* p. 1054; Bright, *Jeremiah,* considers 34:1-7 "a further word from Jeremiah to Zedekiah

vv. 2-7 clearly conform to the B materials and exhibit few features characteristic of C, one should probably ascribe them to the biographical
Jeremianic tradition.[99]

The narrative concerning the manumission of slaves (vv. 8-22) has a
relatively large number of C features. C diction is most frequent in vv.
13-22, which is the speech proper; twelve of the seventeen C phrases, or
71 percent, occur in this section. Several of these, especially in vv. 17ff.,
are conventional curse formulae taken from the stock Deuteronomistic
tradition. The form of this passage is also typical of the C material as a
whole. It is written in a verbose and repetitious style as a sermonic prose
discourse. The theology of C pervades the speech proper.[100] The predicted siege and destruction of Jerusalem are depicted as Yahweh's punishment for the people's breach of the Deuteronomic law of septennial
manumission of Hebrew slaves (Deut 15:1ff.); Zedekiah, the populace in
Jerusalem, and the fathers/ancestors are all accused of disregard for this
law (vv. 14ff.). The option of repentance and conversion is apparently not
offered; the people of God have sealed their fate. According to Nicholson,
the underlying concern of the discourse was again to explain *ex post facto*
why the tragic historical realities of 587 had occurred, while at the same
time to stress the importance of adherence to the law which the ancestors
had failed to obey.[101] To achieve these objectives, Hyatt has argued, the
writer misconstrues an action originally taken for economic and perhaps
military expedience—the manumission of slaves under Zedekiah—as one
enacted in compliance with Deuteronomic law.[102] As for structure, the
speech has been said to conform to the formal Deuteronomistic pattern
underlying several other C passages: (1) introduction, vv. 8-12; (2) the
word of Yahweh in the imperative/the explicit commandments, vv. 13-14;

(vv. 2-5), for which the Biographer was supplied a framework describing
its setting (vv. 1, 6-7)" (p. 217).

[99]Thus, Thiel, *Die deuteronomistische Redaktion, 26-45,* pp. 38f.

[100]Mowinckel, *Komposition,* p. 31; Rudolph, *Jeremia,* pp. xv, 189ff.;
Hyatt, "Deuteronomic Edition," pp. 87f.; *Jeremiah,* 1055ff.; Nicholson,
Preaching, pp. 63ff.; Thiel, *Die deuteronomistische Redaktion, 26-45,* pp.
39ff.; see also Weinfeld, *Deuteronomy and the Deuteronomic School,* p.
103.

[101]Nicholson, *Preaching,* pp. 64f.

[102]Hyatt, *Jeremiah,* p. 1056; "Deuteronomic Edition," pp. 87f.

(3) a statement/description of Israel's disobedience, vv. 14b-16; and (4) an announcement of Yahweh's judgment upon Israel, vv. 17-22.[103]

There is no characteristic C diction at all in vv. 2-7, as we have already indicated. In vv. 1, 8-22 there are seventeen instances, but a relatively large proportion of these (six, or 35 percent) are C+ additions. This leaves eleven in the common text (C'), one in vs. 1 (the introductory formula), one in vs. 8, and nine in the speech proper (vv. 13-22). In this earlier literary stage of the text, however, it is only in the speech proper that diction attested in Dtr (four instances) is to be found. This picture is not greatly changed by the C+ additions; a word is added to vs. 1, creating a Dtr cliché which already had appeared in C' in vs. 17, and another Dtr phrase is created the same way in vs. 18. As is often the case, the rest of the characteristic C diction which C+ adds (four instances) is not attested in Dtr or Deuteronomy. In short, the later expansion of the chapter has not significantly enhanced its likeness to Dtr.

35:1-19

The two text traditions present the narrative account in vv. 1-11 without substantial differences in content or arrangement. The MT has a fuller text than the OG *Vorlage*, and is approximately 19 percent (or seventy-six words) longer. The MT plusses are similar to those found throughout the Jeremianic prose tradition. They expand names and titles to fuller forms (vv. 1, 8, 11), make implicit pronominal suffixes explicit (vs. 5; cf. vs. 11 where an adverb of place is made explicit in the MT), and clarify text (vv. 2, 3, 5, 7, 8).

The same may be said of the two speeches in vv. 12-17, 18f., although here the MT is more heavily expanded and the formulaic introduction to the Rechabite oracle (vs. 12) appears in the third person (to conform with vs. 1?) rather than in autobiographical style as in the OG *Vorlage*.

(1) <u>הדבר אשר–היה אל–ירמיהו מאת יהוה</u> בימי יהויקים
בן–יאשיהו מלך יהודה לאמר: (2) הלוך אל–^xבית הרכבים^x
ודברת אותם והבאותם בית יהוה אל–אחת הלשכות והשקית
אותם יין: (3) ואקח^x את–יאזניה^x בן–ירמיהו^x בן–
חבצניה ואת–אחיו ואת–כל–בניו ואת כל–בית הרכבים:
(4) ואבא אתם בית יהוה אל–לשכת בני חנן בן–יגדליהו^x

[103]Janssen, *Exilszeit*, pp. 105ff.

איש האלהים אשר-אצל לשכת השרים אשר ממעל ללשכת
מעשיהו בן-שלם שמר הסף: (5) ואתן לפני ¹בני בית-
הרכבים¹ גבעים˟ מלאים יין וכסות ואמר אליהם שתו-
יין: (6) ויאמר לא נשתה-יין כי יונדב בן-רכב אבינו
צוה עלינו לאמר לא תשתו-יין אתם ובניכם עד-עולם:
(7) ובית לא-תבנו וזרע לא-תזרעו וכרם לא-תטעו
ולא יהיה לכם כי באהלים תשבו כל-ימיכם למען תחיו
ימים רבים על-פני האדמה אשר אתם גרים שם˟: (8)
ונשמע בקול יהונדב בן-רכב אבינו לכל אשר צונו
לבלתי שתות-יין כל-ימינו אנחנו נשינו˟ בנינו˟
ובנתינו: (9) ולבלתי בנות בתים לשבתנו˟ וכרם
ושדה וזרע לא יהיה-לנו: (10) ונשב באהלים ונשמע
ונעש ככל אשר-צונו יונדב אבינו: (11) ויהי בעלות
נבוכדראצר˟ מלך-בבל אל-˟הארץ ונאמר באו ונבוא
ירושלם מפני חיל הכשדים ומפני חיל ארם˟ ונשב
בירושלם²: (12) ³ויהי דבר-יהוה אל-ירמיהו³ לאמר:
(13) כה-אמר יהוה צבאות אלהי ישראל הלך ואמרת
לאיש יהודה וליושבי ירושלם הלוא תקחו מוסר לשמע
אל-דברי נאם-יהוה (14) ⁴הוקם את-דברי יהונדב⁴ בן-
רכב אשר-צוה את-בניו לבלתי שתות-יין ולא שתו עד-
היום הזה כי שמעו את מצות אביהם ואנכי דברתי
אליכם השכם ודבר ולא שמעתם אלי: (15) ואשלח
אליכם את-כל-עבדי הנבאים השכים ושלח לאמר שבו-
נא˟ איש מדרכו הרעה והיטיבו מעליכם ואל-תלכו
אחרי אלהים אחרים לעבדם ושב אל-˟האדמה אשר-נתתי
לכם ולאבתיכם ולא הטיתם את-אזנכם ולא שמעתם אלי:
(16) כי˟ הקימו בני יהונדב בן-רכב את-מצות אביהם
אשר צום והעם הזה לא שמעו אלי: (17) לכן כה-אמר
יהוה אלהי צבאות אלהי ישראל הנני מביא אל-⁵-יהודה
ואל-⁵ כל-יושבי ירושלם את כל-הרעה אשר דברתי עליהם
יען דברתי אליהם ולא שמעו ואקרא להם ולא ענו (18)
⁶ולבית הרכבים אמר ירמיהו כה-אמר יהוה צבאות אלהי
ישראל יען אשר ⁷שמעתם על-מצות יהונדב אביכם⁷ ותשמרו

---

[1]OG reads *prosōpon autōn*.

[2]OG reads *kai ōkoumen ekei*.

[3]OG reads *kai egeneto logos kuriou pros me*.

[4]OG reads *estēsan hrēma huioi Iōnadab huiou Rēchab*.

[5]OG reads *epi Iouda kai epi . . . .*

[6]OG is much shorter and reads simply *dia touto outōs eipe kurios*.

[7]OG reads *epeidē ēkousan huioi Iōnadab huiou Rēchab tēn entolēn tou patros autōn*.

את-כל-מצותיו ותעשו^x ככל^x אשר-צוה^x אתכם^x: (19)

לכן כה אמר <u>יהוה</u> <u>צבאות אלהי ישראל</u> לא-יכרת איש^x

ליונדב בן-רכב עבד לפני כל-הימים⁸:

		C'	C		C'	C
Type I:	1. (vs. 8)	X	X	5. (vs. 15)	X	X
	3. (vs. 15)	X	X	6. (vs. 15)	X	X
	4. (vs. 15)	X	X	10. (vs. 17)	X*	X*
				12. (vs. 15)	X	X
Type II:	41. (vs. 13)	X	X			
Type IV:	68. (vs. 13)	–	Xc	71. (vs. 1)	X	X
	68. (vs. 17)	–	Xc	72. (vs. 15)	X	X
	68. (vs. 18)	–	Xc	79. (vs. 13)	X	X
	68. (vs. 19)	–	X	82. (vs. 15)	X*	X*
	70. (vs. 14)	X	X	89. (vs. 17)	–	X
	70. (vs. 15)	–	X	91. (vs. 17)	X	X

Summary Tabulation of Instances

	I	II	III	IV	totals
C':	7	1	–	6	14
C+:	–	–	–	6	6
C:	7	1	–	12	20

Although the narrative account begins with the customary introductory C formula (vs. 1) and exhibits the verbose style which is characteristic of this stratum (e.g., vv. 7-9), most of the characteristic C features are found in two speeches later in the chapter (vv. 12-19). Typical C diction is rare in the initial account but frequent in the following discourses. A significantly large proportion appears toward the end of the first of these in vv. 15-17 (twelve of twenty instances, 62 percent).

Duhm argued that this chapter in its present form is the work of a later editor who took as his point of departure a suggestion (*Anregung*) from Baruch's biography.[104] Mowinckel included it in his Deuteronomistic C

---

[104] Duhm, *Das Buch Jeremia,* pp. 284ff.

[8] OG reads *tas hēmeras tēs gēs.*

source on the grounds that the composition employs the typical introductory formula, the expected prose and sermonic style, and the characteristic Deuteronomistic expressions.[105] Moreover, it reflects the same structural pattern shared by other prose sermons in the book (e.g., 7:1ff.; 34:8ff.; 25:1-11a), namely a prophetic summons to repentance and conversion, the identification of the people's wrongdoing, and as a result of the lack of repentance, the inevitable judgment of Yahweh. This pattern appears in 35:1-19 in the sense that the three elements are "illustrated antithetically by means of the conduct of the Rechabites."[106] The prose sermon(s) also reflects several theological motifs of C, such as the deep-seated and recurrent apostasy of the people from Yahweh and his commandments, which is equivalent to idolatry in the writer's opinion (vs. 15). Nicholson has discussed chap. 35 with reference to its literary form and structure;[107] in his view vv. 15ab and 17 set forth the Deuteronomistic *Prophetenaussage* (2 Kgs 17:13ff.), while the chapter as a whole exhibits the covenant form which underlies several sermons and speeches in the Jeremianic and Deuteronomistic literary corpora.[108] Herrmann considered the salvific promise to the Rechabites in vv. 18f. to be Deuteronomistic, and judged the Rechabite belief in Yahweh's ties to the wilderness tradition, as well as their zeal to maintain the purity of Yahwism, to coincide directly with the Deuteronomistic way of thinking (2 Kgs 10:15ff.).[109]

All of the Deuteronomistic indices which have been observed in this chapter are represented fully in C', including all of the instances of diction attested in Dtr (eight), most of which appear in three verses (vv. 15-17, six of eight). (There is no Deuteronomic diction in the chapter which is not also attested in Dtr.) Diction which is not attested in Dtr or Deuteronomy (our Type IV) appears in C' almost as frequently (six instances, as compared to eight), but the number is doubled by the expansions of C+ (to twelve, by adding six). Three of the six have been created by adding to expressions already in the text of C' (vv. 13, 17, 18), and one of the others (vs. 17b) is evidently a gloss from Jeremiah 7:13 which serves here to reinforce the theme of the persistent waywardness of the people and perhaps also to justify the predicted judgment (vs. 17a). In short, the C+

---

[105]Mowinckel, *Komposition*, pp. 31, 34f., 38.

[106]Ibid., pp. 34f.

[107]Nicholson, *Preaching*, pp. 32-34, 55ff.

[108]See pp. 24f. above.

[109]Herrmann, *Heilserwartungen*, pp. 185f.

expansions have significantly multiplied the instances of characteristic C diction in the chapter, but they have not added to the explicitly Deuter-onomistic diction or enhanced the associations with Deuteronomistic tradition.

39:15-18

The MT of this passage is 18 percent (or eleven words) longer than the reconstructed OG *Vorlage*. The MT plusses are similar to those found elsewhere in this corpus. In the section which precedes this passage vv. 4-13 are lacking in the LXX. Most critics consider the LXX to be defective by homoeoteleuton, arguing that the copyist skipped from מלך בבל at the end of vs. 3 to the same words at the end of vs. 13.[110] While this is con-ceivable, the expansionistic *Tendenz* of the MT of Jeremiah and the clearly secondary nature of vv. 4-10 have led Janzen to conclude that the OG may witness to an earlier reading of the text.[111]

(15) ואל-ירמיהו היה דבר-יהוה בהיתו עצור בחצר
המטרה לאמר: (16) הלוך ואמרת לעבד-מלך הכושי
לאמר כה-אמר יהוה צבאות אלהי ישראל הנני מבי
את-דברי אל^X-העיר הזאת לרעה ולא לטובה והיו
לפניך ביום ההוא: (17) והצלתיך ביום-ההוא נאם-
יהוה ולא תנתן^X ביד האנשים אשר-אתה יגור
מפניהם: (18) כי מלט אמלטך ובחרב לא תפל
והיתה לך נפשך לשלל כי-בטח בי נאם-יהוה:

		C'	C		C'	C
Type IV:	68. (vs. 16)		-			Xc

---

[110]For example, Rudolph, *Jeremia*; "39:4-13 fehlt in G, aber nur durch Homoioteleuton . . ." (p. 209); Bright, *Jeremiah*, p. 245; Hyatt, *Jeremiah*; "the LXX omits vv. 4-13 either because most of the material is contained in ch. 52, or simply by accident . . ." (p. 1079).

[111]Janzen, *Studies*, p. 118.

Summary Tabulation of Instances

	I	II	III	IV	totals
C':	-	-	-	-	-
C+:	-	-	-	1	1
C:	-	-	-	1	1

Although 39:15-18 has only one instance of characteristic C diction (vs. 16), it has often been included in the C corpus and associated with Deuteronomic tradition. Duhm contended that this brief passage is the work of a later supplementor.[112] He maintained that the editor could not let Ebedmelech's deed (reported in 38:7-13) go unmentioned, without composing a word of Yahweh about him. His composition is couched in language which is similar to that employed in other supplementary pieces (cf. vs. 16 רעה and טובה + (H) בא with 19:15 and 21:10). Mowinckel included 39:15-18 among other Deuteronomistic C materials on the grounds that it interrupts the continuity between 39:14 and 40:2 (which are B materials) and exhibits the style and customary title of the C source.[113] Against Rudolph, who ascribes this passage to Baruch,[114] Hyatt has argued that vv. 15-18 are from a Deuteronomic editor because of the Deuteronomic doctrine of retribution which he detects in the reward Ebedmelech receives for his act of kindness towards Jeremiah.[115]

The one characteristic C phrase (vs. 16) belongs to the C+ expansion, and the introductory formula (vs. 15) is worded differently from other C passages. The passage may be secondary from a literary point of view, but there is little basis for associating it with the C corpus as it appears in the common text (C') or even as it appears in the MT.

44:1-14

The MT of this section again reflects a more developed text. It is 19 percent (or fifty words) longer than the reconstructed OG *Vorlage*. Janzen has shown that the majority of the MT plusses are glosses introduced from parallel and related contexts, or derived from the conflation of variant

---

[112]Duhm, *Das Buch Jeremia*, pp. 312f.

[113]Mowinckel, *Komposition*, pp. 40, 44.

[114]Rudolph, *Jeremia*, pp. xiv, 210ff.

[115]Hyatt, *Jeremiah*, pp. 1081-83.

readings.[116] There are a number of short additions (e.g., vv. 2, 3, 4, passim) and one longer expansion (vv. 11f.). These extend formulaic expressions (vv. 2, 7, 11), fill out pejorative serial clauses (vv. 12, 13) and stock phrases (vv. 3, 10, 11), and supply clarifying glosses (vv. 3, 9, 14). Except for the addition of ובנף (vs. 1), the MT plusses do not introduce new subject matter to C'.

(1) הדבר אשר היה אל־ירמיהו אל כל־היהודים הישבים
בארץ מצרים הישבים^X במגדל ובתחפנחס ובנף ובארץ
פתרוס לאמר: (2) כה־אמר יהוה צבאות אלהי ישראל
אתם ראיתם את כל־הרעה אשר הבאתי על־ירושלם ועל
כל־ערי יהודה והנם חרבה היום הזה ואין^X בהם יושב:
(3) מפני רעתם אשר עשו להכעסני ללכת לקטר לעבד
לאלהים אחרים אשר לא ידעום^X המה אתם ואבתיכם: (4)
ואשלח אליכם את־כל־עבדי הנביאים השכים ושלח^X לאמר
אל־נא^X תעשו את דבר־התעבה הזאת אשר שנאתי: (5)
ולא שמעו^X ולא־הטו את־אזנם לשוב מרעתם לבלתי קטר
לאלהים אחרים: (6) ותתך חמתי ואפי ותבער בערי
יהודה ובחצות ירושלם ותהיינה לחרבה לשממה כיום
הזה: (7) ועתה כה־אמר יהוה אלהי צבאות אלהי ישראל
למה אתם עשים רעה גדולה אל^X־נפשתכם להכרית
לכם איש־ואשה עולל ויונק מתוך יהודה לבלתי הותיר
לכם שארית: (8) להכעסני במעשי ידיכם לקטר לאלהים
אחרים בארץ מצרים אשר־אתם^X באים^X לגור שם למען
הכרית לכם ולמען היותכם לקללה ולחרפה בכל גויי
הארץ: (9) השכחתם את־רעות אבותיכם ואת־רעות מלכי
יהודה ואת רעות נשיו^X [1]ואת רעתכם^X ואת רעת^X נשיכם
אשר עשו בארץ יהודה ובחצות ירושלם: (10) לא^X דכאו^X
עד היום הזה ולא יראו ולא־הלכו בתורתי ובחקתי
אשר־נתתי לפניכם ולפני אבותיכם^X: (11) לכן כה־
אמר יהוה צבאות אלהי ישראל הנני שם פני בכם לרעה
ולהכרית את־כל־יהודה: (12) ולקחתי את־שארית יהודה
אשר־שמו פניהם לבוא ארץ־מצרים לגור שם ותמו כל
בארץ^X מצרים יפלו^X בחרב ברעב יתמו מקטן ועד־גדול
בחרב וברעב ימתו והיו לאלה[2] לשמה ולקללה ולחרפה:
(13) ופקדתי על היושבים בארץ מצרים כאשר פקדתי על־

---

[116]Janzen, *Studies*, pp. 17-19, 25, 57f.

[1]May be omitted in OG by haplography.
[2]May be omitted in OG by haplography.

ירושלם בַחֶרֶב בָּרָעָב[X] וּמַדְבֵּר: (14) וְלֹא יִהְיֶה פָּלִיט
וְשָׂרִיד לִשְׁאֵרִית יְהוּדָה הַבָּאִים לָגוּר[X]-שָׁם בְּאֶרֶץ מִצְרַיִם
וְלָשׁוּב[X] אֶרֶץ יְהוּדָה אֲשֶׁר-הֵמָּה מְנַשְּׂאִים אֶת-נַפְשָׁם לָשׁוּב
לָשֶׁבֶת שָׁם כִּי לֹא-יָשׁוּבוּ כִּי אִם-פְּלֵטִים:

		C'	C		C'	C
Type I:	5. (vs. 4)	X	X	8. (vs. 8)	X	X
	6. (vs. 3)	-	X	14. (vs. 6)	X	X
	7. (vs. 3)	X	X	20. (vs. 4)	X	X
Type II:	38. (vs. 3)	X	X	39. (vs. 6)	X	X
	38. (vs. 5)	X	X	39. (vs. 8)	X	X
	38. (vs. 8)	X	X	39. (vs. 12)	X	X
				45. (vs. 10)	-	Xc
Type III:	55. (vs. 3)	X	X			
Type IV:	68. (vs. 2)	-	Xc	69. (vs. 13)	-	Xc
	68. (vs. 7)	-	Xc	70. (vs. 4)	X	X
	68. (vs. 11)	-	Xc	72. (vs. 5)	X	X
	69. (vs. 12)	X*	X*	74. (vs. 6)	X	X
	69. (vs. 12)	-	X*	76. (vs. 13)	X	X
				76. (vs. 13)	X	X

Summary Tabulation of Instances

	I	II	III	IV	totals
C':	5	6	1	6	18
C+:	1	1	-	5	7
C:	6	7	1	11	25

Most commentators and critics have recognized that Jeremiah 44 in its present form is composed of more than one literary stratum (or traditionary complex or editorial unit). According to Duhm, vv. 1-14, 20-23, 27, 29f. are the work of a later supplementor, while vv. 15-19, 24-25, 28b are the revised portion of an older source (Baruch's book).[117] Mowinckel argued that vv. 1-14 (which he ascribed to C) have been inserted in a biographical account in 43:8-13 and 44:15-19 and have consequently

[117]Duhm, *Das Buch Jeremia,* pp. 327ff.

destroyed its formal and factual continuity.[118] Leslie and Rudolph have assigned Jeremiah 44 as a whole to Baruch, although both detect indications of Deuteronomistic editorial activity.[119] Hyatt held that the chapter had been rewritten by the Deuteronomistic editor of the book; it rests "upon authentic words of Jeremiah, preserved in Baruch's memoirs, but the phrasing is D's and the theme is a favorite of his."[120] Thiel has recently contended that vv. 1-14, 20-23 are the product of the Deuteronomistic redactor of Jeremiah and that vv. 15-19, 24ff. are part of an older source which the redactor has reworked,[121] an analysis similar to Duhm's.

Although several sources have been ascertained in chapter 44 as a whole, vv. 1-14 have most frequently been reckoned to exhibit characteristics associated with the C material and Deuteronomistic tradition. Duhm saw in these verses the repetitious and stereotyped Deuteronomistic diction which frequently appears in the speeches of the "pseudo-Jeremiah," and he thought the theological perspective to be virtually identical, except that in 44:1ff. the focus is upon the Jews who had migrated to Egypt.[122] These emigrants are threatened with the same fate which befell the inhabitants of Jerusalem because of their incessant idolatry (serving foreign gods). (Duhm also observed that the supplementor or editor of vv. 1-14 attached his material to an older and more important [historical] source; in a manner analogous to the editor[s] of the books of Kings, he composed his work freely to support and interpret this earlier report [vv. 15-19]). Mowinckel discerned in 44:1-14 several ideas and

---

[118]Mowinckel, *Komposition,* pp. 10ff., 31, 50. With respect to vv. 20-23, Mowinckel asserted that they "are admittedly an insertion of a pedant who would not have tolerated the man of God holding a long conversation with women" (p. 10); see also *Prophecy and Tradition,* p. 22.

[119]Rudolph, *Jeremia,* pp. 223f.; Leslie, *Jeremiah,* pp. 283f. Leslie regarded vv. 3-6, 9-14 to be the product of the Deuteronomistic editor, because they reflect his style and theology.

[120]Hyatt, *Jeremiah,* pp. 1096ff.; "Deuteronomic Edition," p. 89.

[121]Thiel, *Die deuteronomistische Redaktion,* 26-45, pp. 69f.

[122]Duhm, *Das Buch Jeremia,* pp. 328ff. In his discussion of the theological perspective of 44:1ff., Duhm commented: "From speeches of the pseudo-Jeremiah, it should not be concluded that these discourses must belong to the actual Deuteronomistic period (up to Ezra); they only demonstrate that for the devotionally popular storyteller, Deuteronomy and the writings dependent on it supplied much more stimulation and profit than the more tedious and technical priestly codes" (p. 329).

motifs which are characteristic of the C corpus as a whole;[123] the sermon blatantly condemns the Jews in Egypt for their cultic apostasy, serving and burning incense to other gods—sins, it believes, that have character-ized the entire historical experience of the people of God (vs. 9)—and depicts the role and function of the prophet in a thoroughly Deuteronomic light. The perception of the prophet which emerges is that of a sentry who warns the people against idolatry and other covenant regulations of Yah-weh's law, namely Deuteronomy. He is, moreover, a member of a long institutional line of prophets who have borne the same message, admon-ishing the people not to commit idolatry and serving as custodians of Yahweh's commandments. According to Hyatt, this chapter abounds in Deuteronomistic diction and ideas and reflects the prolix and repetitious style which is typical of D.[124] Furthermore, vv. 2-20 provide an excellent summary of the Deuteronomistic theology of history "with an exaggerated statement of the destruction wrought in Judah and emphasis on the repeated warning which had been sent through the prophets, ending with a general condemnation for disobedience and false worship."[125] Nicholson has treated Jeremiah 44 as part of a larger narrative complex contained in chapters 40:7-44:30. These chapters, he argues, do not constitute a passion narrative (*Leidensgeschichte*) or part of Baruch's memoirs, as has been generally assumed. Rather, they supply an explanation of the fate of those who had remained in Judah (שארית) after the devastation of Jerusa-lem. Jeremiah 44 and the material that precedes it (in 40:7-43:13) assert that "the future of Israel lay with the Babylonian diaspora and like [chap-ter] xxiv but with even greater intensity [polemize] against the Egyptian diaspora during the exilic period."[126]

In this passage there are twenty-five instances of the characteristic C diction we have indexed. This is a relatively large number, almost twice the number of verses. A relatively large proportion of these represent diction attested in Dtr (thirteen, or 52 percent). The earlier literary stage of the text (C') lacks some of the verbosity and repetition of the later stage, as we have already noted, and it also lacks seven of the instances of characteristic C diction. These include only two of the expressions attested in Dtr, however; the five others are of the type not attested in Dtr or Deuteronomy (our Type IV). This means that C' has fewer instances

---

[123]Mowinckel, *Komposition*, pp. 10ff., 31, 50.

[124]Hyatt, *Jeremiah*, p. 1096.

[125]Ibid.

[126]Nicholson, *Preaching*, p. 111.

of characteristic C diction, but a larger proportion of its clichés are attested in Dtr (61 percent). The C+ expansions have added phrases which can be found in other C passages, but few which are attested in Dtr.

45:1-5

The MT and OG *Vorlage* represent this brief oracle concerning Baruch, Jeremiah's scribe, with few variations. The MT is a slightly fuller text; it has filled out the prophetic formula in vs. 2 with an additional epithet and expanded vs. 4 with the phrase ואת-כל-הארץ היא, apparently to stress the predicted destruction. It is interesting that both witnesses reflect the same corruption in vs. 3. Bright has observed that the words תאמר אליו are "superfluous and inappropriate in the immediate context."[127] Janzen has concluded from this and other similar corruptions common to the MT and OG *Vorlage* that one "must suppose an appreciable lapse of time between the redaction of the book and the divergence of the two text traditions."[128]

(1) הדבר אשר דבר ירמיהו הנביא אל-ברוך בן-נריה
בכתבו את-הדברים האלה על-ᵡספר מפי ירמיהו בשנה
הרבעית ליהויקים בן-יאשיהו מלך יהודה לאמר: (2)
כה-אמר יהוה אלהי ישראל עליך ברוך: (3) אמרתᵡ
אוי-נאᵡ ליᵡ כי-יסף יהוה יגון על-מכאביᵡ יגעתי
באנחתיᵡ ומנוחה לא מצאתי: (4) כה תאמר אליו כה
אמר יהוה הנה אשרᵡ בניתי אני הרם ואת אשר-ᵡ
נטעתי נתש ואת-כל-הארץ היא: (5) ואתה תבקש-לך
גדלות אל-תבקש כי הנני מביא רעה על-כל-בשר נאם-
יהוה ונתתי לך את-נפשך לשלל עלᵡ כל-המקמותᵡ
אשר תלך-שם:

		C'	C		C'	C
Type I:	10. (vs. 5)	X	X			
Type IV:	86. (vs. 4)	X	X			

---

[127]Bright, *Jeremiah*, p. 184.
[128]Janzen, *Studies*, p. 134.

Summary Tabulation of Instances

	I	II	III	IV	totals
C':	1	-	-	1	2
C+:	-	-	-	-	-
C:	1	-	-	1	2

Scholars have been divided in their assessment of Jer 45:1-5. While Duhm, Rudolph and others[129] have assigned the passage to B because of its stylistic affinity with other passages in this block of material, Mowinckel, Hyatt, Nicholson, and Thiel regard at least parts of it as Deuteronomistic. Most of the arguments of the latter critics are admittedly weak and seem to be based more on analogy and the process of elimination than on substantial evidence. Mowinckel admitted that 45:1-5 deviates from the customary C materials in its heading, content, and style, and noted that the passage is an oracle and not a speech in the usual style of C; but he reasoned that it is the formal conclusion of R^{ABC} (the redactor who added source C and other materials to the book) and thus is probably to be reckoned to the Deuteronomistic C source.[130] (In *Prophecy and Tradition*, Mowinckel revised this judgment and ascribed the chapter to Baruch.[131]) Although he found this oracle to be basically authentic, Hyatt assigned it to a Deuteronomistic editor in view of a few phrases in vv. 4-5b and the Deuteronomistic doctrine of retribution, which could not allow the faithful service of Baruch to go unrewarded (vs. 5).[132]

The few characteristic C features which have been seen in the passage are represented fully in C'.

---

[129]For example, Leslie, *Jeremiah*, pp. 183f.

[130]Mowinckel, *Komposition*, pp. 44f.

[131]Mowinckel, *Prophecy and Tradition*, pp. 61f.

[132]Hyatt, "Deuteronomic Edition," p. 89; *Jeremiah*, pp. 1101ff.

4

A Comparative Analysis
of Correspondences in Diction

The differences which we have observed between the longer text of C (=MT) and the shorter text of C' bear more directly, and more clearly, upon matters of diction than upon any of the other kinds of association with the Deuteronomistic tradition. Although we have examined the theological, stylistic, and formal differences between the texts, these indices are not as readily tabulated because they are more complex observations and often more particular to the views of individual researchers. It is therefore primarily the indices of diction which we now propose to analyze more precisely.

The nineteen passages we have analyzed vary a great deal in length as well as in the nature and number of characteristic C features they exhibit. To have a valid basis for comparison we need some way to take this difference in length into account. Any choice will be somewhat arbitrary, but for our purposes any reasonable method will serve; we cannot claim that any of the numerical data we offer in this chapter provide exact measurements in any event. We have decided to count the words of each passage, and to reckon as a "word" all Hebrew morphemes or combinations of morphemes, including those joined by a *maqqēp,* which are not separated by a space in the BHS edition of the MT. We recognize that the use of *maqqēp* is not entirely consistent, and that identical phrases sometimes appear with it and sometimes without it, but we believe that this slight irregularity is more than offset by the advantage of having a method which is simple to apply and to verify. Measured in this way, the nineteen passages vary from 711 (32:1-44) to 62 (39:15-18) words, so the longest is more than eleven times the shortest. Eight are less than 200 words, six are more than 400, five fall between. The following table lists the passages in order of length, together with our word count:

TABLE 1

THE PASSAGES OF THE PUTATIVE C CORPUS
RANKED BY LENGTH

1)	32:1-44	(711)*	11)	11:1-14	(239)
2)	7:1-8:3	(584)	12)	19:2b-9,	
				11b-13	(178)
3)	29:1-32	(523)	13)	21:1-10	(177)
4)	27:1-22	(402)	14)	17:19-27	(167)*
5)	33:1-26	(402)*	15)	18:1-12	(148)*
6)	34:1-22	(401)*	16)	3:6-13	(135)
7)	35:1-19	(356)*	17)	45:1-5	(89)
8)	16:1-15	(268)	18)	22:1-5	(85)
9)	44:1-14	(266)	19)	39:15-18	(62)
10)	25:1-14	(242)			

total: 5435

In several cases these passages follow one another directly in the book of Jeremiah, so they really form larger blocks of continuous C material. Those which are joined in this way with other passages are marked with an asterisk. 17:19-27 (167 words) is followed directly by 18:1-12 (148 words), making a passage of 315 words. 32:1-44 (711 words), 33:1-26 (402 words), 34:1-22 (401 words) and 35:1-19 (356 words) also follow one another directly, making a long continuous block of 1870 words; this is by far the longest section of continuous C material in the book, and in fact 34 percent of the entire C corpus.

We shall begin our analysis with the text of C (the expanded text as it appears in the MT) in order to have a basis for comparison, and then proceed to C' (the common text) and C+ (the additions to the common text).[1] In the last section we shall consider other changes which C+ additions have introduced to C'.

DEUTERONOMISTIC DICTION IN THE
READINGS OF C (= MT)

In these passages we have identified 312 instances of indexed words and phrases. How these are distributed among our four types of diction, and the percentage of the total which each type represents, can be seen in the following table:

---

[1] The present study focuses upon additions in the MT. Additions in the OG hardly ever bear upon the question at hand.

TABLE 2

INSTANCES OF INDEXED DICTION IN THE C CORPUS

types of diction:	I	II	III	IV	total
number of instances:	93	50	35	134	312
percentage of total:	30%	16%	11%	43%	(100%)

As is immediately evident, Type III diction is the smallest percentage of the total, indicating that C uses relatively little language found in Deuteronomy which is not also employed by Dtr. The most frequent is Type IV, comparable to the combined total of Types I and II (46 percent), that is, all diction attested in Dtr. It appears, then, that diction similar to Dtr but not actually attested there is approximately as common as diction actually attested in Dtr (43 percent and 46 percent of the total, respectively). This might suggest that C is a step removed from Dtr; as we proceed to analyze our findings, we will want to keep this question in mind.

Table 2 counts each use of an indexed word or phrase as one instance, without taking into account the number of words involved. In order to find out what percentage of the total language of the corpus is represented by indexed language, we need to count the number of indexed words and compare this to the total number of words in the passage.

TABLE 3

PERCENTAGE OF THE C TEXT IDENTIFIED
AS INDEXED DICTION

total number of words in the C corpus:				5435	100%
number of words in the indexed diction:				1055	19%

by type:	I	295 words	5%
	II	162 words	3%
	III	145 words	3%
	IV	453 words	8%

The density of indexed diction (19 percent) is sufficiently high to warrant the supposition of some sort of association. Otherwise, results are comparable to Table 2; there is little Deuteronomic diction not already used by Dtr (Type III), and Type IV is about equal to I and II.

The number of instances of indexed diction (Table 2) can be compared to the number of indices to see how often, on the average, these various indexed words and phrases appear in the corpus. In the following table, the "number of indices" means the number of different words or phrases employed, as listed in our catalog in chap. 2.

TABLE 4

AVERAGE FREQUENCY OF INDEXED WORDS AND PHRASES IN C

types of diction:	I	II	III	IV	(total)
a. number of instances:	93	50	35	134	(312)
b. number of indices:	37	13	17	25	(92)
average frequency (a. divided by b.)	2.5	3.8	2.1	5.4	(3.4)

As the table indicates, indexed words and phrases attested in Deuteronomy but not in Dtr (Type III) have the lowest average frequency. The indexed words and phrases which have the highest average frequency are those which are similar to Dtr (or Deuteronomy) but not actually attested there (Type IV). In interpreting these data it must be kept in mind that most of the words and phrases we have included in our catalog of Type IV diction occur in the corpus at least three times, so the average for this category will not be much less than 3.0 in any event. It is nevertheless to be noted that the average frequency is nearly double that, and markedly higher than the average frequency of Types I and II combines (143 divided by 50, or 2.9).

What has just been observed about the C corpus as a whole does not hold true consistently for each passage. In fact there is rather wide variation. To illustrate this we list below the nineteen passages, and give for each the number of instances of indexed language, the number of different indexed words or phrases to be found, and the percentage of the total number of words which indexed language represents. Note in particular that the percentage of indexed language varies from 34 percent to 6 percent, which indicates that such diction is not distributed very evenly through the passages which have been generally regarded as C material. Five of the nineteen passages have 11 percent indexed language or less, while five others have 25 percent or more.

TABLE 5

INDEXED LANGUAGE IN C, BY PASSAGE

passage	number of instances	number of indices	% of total number of words
3:6-13	4	4	10%
7:1-8-3	55	41	34%
11:1-14	26	19	34%
16:1-15	17	14	32%
17:19-27	8	8	15%
18:1-12	9	8	21%
19:2b-9 11b-13	13	12	29%
21:1-10	8	7	16%
22:1-5	4	4	22%
25:1-14	17	14	24%
27:1-22	15	10	10%
29:1-32	21	15	11%
32:1-44	38	35	16%
33:1-26	12	8	10%
34:1-22	17	13	15%
35:1-19	20	16	18%
39:15-18	1	1	6%
44:1-14	25	16	26%
45:1-5	2	2	12%

In a separate table we offer an analysis of these figures according to the four types of diction we have distinguished. We have observed (in Table 2) that for C materials as a whole Type IV diction appears about as often as Types I and II combined, but there is a rather wide variation from passage to passage.

TABLE 6

INDEXED LANGUAGE IN C, BY PASSAGE AND TYPE

passage and type diction	number of instances	number of indices	% of total number of words
3:6-13			
I:	4	4	10%
7:1-8:3			
I:	17	13	10%
II:	10	7	6%
III:	6	6	4%
IV:	22	15	14%
11:1-14			
I:	9	7	13%
II:	10	5	8%
III:	3	3	6%
IV:	4	4	7%
16:1-15			
I:	6	4	9%
II:	2	2	3%
III:	4	4	12%
IV:	5	4	8%
17:19-27			
I:	1	1	1%
II:	2	2	7%
IV:	5	5	6%
18:1-12			
I:	3	3	5%
II:	1	1	3%
IV:	5	4	12%
19:2b-9 11b-13			
I:	2	2	4%
II:	4	4	8%
III:	3	3	8%
IV:	4	3	8%

TABLE 6 (Continued)

passage and type diction	number of instances	number of indices	% of total number of words
21:1-10			
I:	1	1	2%
III:	2	2	5%
IV:	5	4	10%
22:1-5			
I:	1	1	5%
III:	1	1	4%
IV:	2	2	13%
25:1-14			
I:	7	6	10%
II:	2	1	3%
III:	1	1	1%
IV:	7	6	10%
27:1-22			
II:	1	1	1%
IV:	14	9	10%
29:1-32			
I:	4	4	2%
II:	1	1	1%
III:	4	3	2%
IV:	12	7	6%
32:1-44			
I:	17	16	6%
II:	6	6	3%
III:	4	4	2%
IV:	11	9	5%
33:1-26			
I:	3	3	3%
II:	1	1	1%
III:	3	1	1%
IV:	5	3	4%
34:1-22			
I:	4	3	4%
II:	2	2	2%
III:	3	3	3%
IV:	8	5	7%

TABLE 6 (Continued)

passage and type diction	number of instances	number of indices	% of total number of words
35:1-19			
I:	7	7	6%
II:	1	1	1%
IV:	12	8	11%
39:15-18			
IV:	1	1	6%
44:1-14			
I:	6	6	4%
II:	7	3	8%
III:	1	1	1%
IV:	11	6	12%
45:1-5			
I:	1	1	3%
IV:	1	1	9%

From the list of types of diction (column one), it can be observed that twelve of the nineteen passages employ both Type III and Type IV diction in addition to diction attested in Dtr (Type I or II or both). As one might expect, it is the shorter passages (less than 200 words) which tend to lack one or more of these four types (the only exception is 19:2b-9, 11b-13, which employs them all). Longer passages employ all four types (here the only exception is 27:1-22, 402 words, which lacks Types I and III). Type III is the one most often lacking (lacking in seven passages), and Type IV the least often (lacking in only one passage). Type I is lacking in two passages, Type II in five, but only one passage (39:15-18) lacks them both.

The passages vary greatly in the number of indices they employ (third column) and the number of instances in which these are used (second column), but this is also largely the result of their differences in length. The data given in the last column take this difference into account, because they represent the percentage of the total language of each passage which each type of diction represents. It is significant that Type IV diction constitutes more than half of the indexed language of eight passages (18:1-12; 21:1-10; 22:1-5; 27:1-22; 29:1-32; 35:1-19; 39:15-18, which employs only Type IV; and 45:1-5), while Types I and II together constitute more than half of the indexed language of only five passages

(3:6-13, which employs only Type I; 11:1-14; 17:19-27; 25:1-14; and 32:1-44).

The results are similar if we look for unusually high or low percentages. Type IV diction constitutes 10 percent or more of the language of eight passages (7:1-8:3; 18:1-12; 21:1-10; 22:1-5; 25:1-14; 27:1-22; 35:1-19; and 44:1-14), while Types I and II together bulk this large in six (3:6-13; 7:1-8:3; 11:1-14; 19:2b-9, 11b-13; 25:1-14 and 44:1-14), and Type III only in one (16:1-15). On the other hand, Type IV diction constitutes less than 5 percent of the language of only two passages (33:1-26; and 3:6-13, which has none), while this is true of Types I and II in six (21:1-10; 27:1-22; 29:1-32; 33:1-26; 39:15-18, which has none; and 45:1-5), and of Type III in fifteen passages (of which seven have none).

In summary, while there is rather wide variation between passages, it is Type IV diction which is least often lacking, which most often constitutes more than half of the indexed language, which most often constitutes 10 percent or more of the total language, and least often constitutes less than 5 percent of the total language. Taking the passages as a whole, indexed language in the C corpus is predominantly Type IV. This corroborates what we have already observed in Tables, 2, 3 and 4 and suggests that C is indeed a step removed from Dtr; it often employs diction similar to Dtr but not actually attested there.

Tables 4 and 5 raise another issue as well, because they indicate that these nineteen passages do not constitute a particularly well-unified corpus, at least in terms of the diction we have indexed. To the extent that one defines the corpus as a body of materials which are significantly influenced by diction attested in Dtr or at least similar to it, one would have to regard at least one passage as doubtful (39:15-18) because only 6 percent of its language represents such diction. If the definition is narrowed to those which have diction actually attested in Dtr, then 39:15-18 would have to be excluded from the corpus, because it has none, and others would have to be regarded as doubtful: 21:1-10, where only 2 percent of the language is Dtr diction, and 27:1-22, 29:1-32, 33:1-26, and 45:1-5, all of which have less than 5 percent. It should also be noted that the overall frequency of indexed words in a chapter as a whole does not always give an entirely accurate picture. In 29:1-32, for example, there is a concentration of indexed words in vv. 17-21 (32 percent of the total number of these verses), although the percentage of indexed diction for the chapter as a whole is only 11 percent. Such concentrations of indexed diction may suggest an editorial hand in a specifically limited section (see below for a discussion of C' and C+/C).

DEUTERONOMISTIC DICTION IN THE READINGS OF C'

C', the text common to the OG *Vorlage* and the MT, is the *ante quem* text; that is to say, it represents a stage in the literary history of the corpus prior to the divergence of the textual tradition into two collateral branches. In the tables that follow, we will be comparing C' with C. It is helpful to begin by comparing the length of the text of C' to that of C, and to express this as a ratio.

TABLE 7

COMPARATIVE LENGTHS OF TEXT (C', C AND C+)

comparative lengths of text:	C'	C	C+
total number of words:	4334	5435	1101
percentage of C':	100%	125%	25%
comparative ratio:	3.94	4.94	1.00

NOTE: The comparative ratio is derived by dividing the total number of words in C' and C, respectively, by the total number of words in C+.

The difference in length between C' and C varies a great deal from passage to passage, as the following table indicates. The passages are listed here in the order in which they appear in Table 1, to facilitate comparison. Note that the percentages by which the text of C exceeds that of C' vary from 0 to 94 percent.

TABLE 8

COMPARISON OF PASSAGES IN C' AND C
ACCORDING TO LENGTH

rank in Table 1	locus	words in C	words in C'	words in C+	words in C+ as % of words in C'
1.	32:1-44	711	638	73	11%
2.	7:1-8:3	584	526	58	11%
3.	29:1-32	523	331	192	58%
4.	27:1-22	402	232	170	73%
5.	33:1-26	402	207	195	94%
6.	34:1-22	401	325	76	23%
7.	35:1-19	356	287	69	24%
8.	16:1-15	268	243	25	10%
9.	44:1-14	266	216	50	23%
10.	25:1-14	242	172	70	41%
11.	11:1-14	239	199	40	20%
12.	19:2b-9, 11b-13	178	166	12	7%
13.	21:1-10	177	156	21	13%
14.	17:19-27	167	164	3	2%
15.	18:1-12	148	130	18	14%
16.	3:6-13	135	125	10	8%
17.	45:1-5	89	81	8	10%
18.	22:1-5	85	85	0	-
19.	39:15-18	62	51	11	22%

We have identified 230 instances in which indexed words or phrases are employed in C'. The following table shows how these are distributed by type, and compares these data with those given for C in Table 2. The actual number of instances is given first. Then the number of instances in C' is weighted by multiplying them by 1.25; this makes comparision easier, since it takes into account the difference in the lengths of the texts. Finally, the distribution by type is expressed as a percentage of the total number of instances in each text.

TABLE 9

INSTANCES OF INDEXED DICTION IN C' AND C

types of diction:	I	II	III	IV	total
number of instances:					
C':	83	44	26	78	230
C:	93	50	35	134	312
number of instances weighted according to 3.94:4.94 ration of C':C					
C':	103*	55*	33*	98*	289*
C:	93	50	35	134	312
percentage of total					
C':	36%	19%	11%	34%	100%
C:	30%	16%	11%	43%	100%

The relatively small percentage of Type III diction indicates that C' and C alike use comparatively little language found in Deuteronomy which is not attested in Dtr. In other respects, however, the distribution in C' is moderately different. While C employs Type IV diction most frequently (134 instances), almost as often as Types I and II combined (143 instances), C' employs Type I diction most frequently (82 instances), and in C' the total of the instances of Types I and II diction (126) is far greater than the instances of Type IV diction (78). Expressed as percentages, 55 percent of the indexed diction in C' is attested in Dtr, whereas this is true of only 46 percent of the indexed diction in C. When the number of instances in C' is weighted to take account of the difference in lengths of the texts, it can be seen that Types I and II are actually more frequent per unit of text in C' than in C (158é compared to 143), even though indexed diction as a whole is slightly more frequent in C (312 compared to 289é). In summary, diction attested in Dtr is more frequent in C', while diction similar to Dtr but not actually attested there is more frequent in C.

If we calculate the percentage of the total language of C' which indexed diction represents, it can be seen that this is comparable to what we have reckoned for C in Table 3:

TABLE 10

PERCENTAGE OF C' TEXT IDENTIFIED
AS INDEXED DICTION

total number of words in C':	4334	100%
(total number of words in C:	5435	100%)
number of words identifed as indexed diction in C':	795	18.3%
(number of words identified as indexed diction in C:	1055	19.4%)

These are virtually identical; a difference of 1 percent is too small to be significant. We believe this warrants the conclusion that there is some form of association between C' and Dtr; in fact, in view of the higher percentage of Types I and II diction, this association is even more evident in C' than in C.

The following table computes the average number of times the indexed words or phrases appear in C', and compares this with the data we have given for C in Table 4:

TABLE 11

AVERAGE FREQUENCY OF INDEXED WORDS
AND PHRASES IN C' AND C

types of diction:					(total)
a. number of instances in C':	82	44	26	78	(230)
in C:	93	50	35	134	(312)
b. number of indices in C':	35	13	16	22	(86)
in C:	37	13	17	25	(92)
average frequency (a. divided by b.)					
in C':	2.3	3.4	1.6	3.5	(2.7)
in C:	2.5	3.8	2.1	5.4	(3.4)

The comparison shows that C' employs almost as many different indexed words and phrases as C (see "number of indices"). The average number of times C' and C employ words or phrases we have cataloged as Types I, II, or III is also comparable. The most obvious difference is again in Type IV diction; C employs twenty-five different words or phrases an average of 5.4 times each, while C' employs twenty-two different words or phrases an average of 3.5 times each. Since we have included in our catalog of Type IV diction only those expressions which occur at least three times in C, this is a significantly low average. It is apparent from this table and Table 9 above that many of the instances of Type IV diction derive from subsequent expansion and not from the text of C'. In short, taking the corpus as a whole, C' seems to be more directly related to Dtr than C.

An analysis of the indexed diction in C' by passage shows the same wide variation we have already observed in C (Table 5). Note that the percentage of the language of the passages which is indexed diction varies from 33% to none; in this respect the corpus is no more homogeneous in C'. A comparison with the data given for C indicates that this percentage is slightly higher in C' for three passages (3:6-13; 25:1-14; 45:1-5), but is significantly lower for three others (27:1-22; 29:1-32; 39:15-18) which have a small percentage in C.

TABLE 12

INDEXED LANGUAGE IN C', BY PASSAGE

passage	number of instances		number of indices		% of total number of words	
	C'	C	C'	C	C'	C
3:6-13	4	4	4	4	12%	10%
7:1-8:3	49	55	46	41	33%	34%
11:1-14	20	26	13	19	33%	34%
16:1-15	14	17	11	14	31%	32%
17:19-27	8	8	8	8	15%	15%
18:1-12	7	9	6	8	18%	21%
19:2b-9						
11b-13	11	13	10	12	27%	28%
21:1-10	6	8	5	7	15%	16%
22:1-5	4	4	4	4	22%	22%
25:1-14	13	17	10	14	25%	24%

TABLE 12 (Continued)

passage	number of instances		number of indices		% of total number of words	
	C'	C	C'	C	C'	C
27:1-22	6	15	3	10	5%	10%
29:1-32	5	21	5	15	3%	11%
32:1-44	32	38	31	35	15%	16%
33:1-26	6	12	5	8	9%	10%
34:1-22	11	17	10	13	14%	15%
35:1-19	14	20	13	16	15%	18%
39:15-18	0	1	0	1	-	6%
44:1-14	18	25	12	16	20%	26%
45:1-5	2	2	2	2	14%	12%
	230	312	92			

The following table analyzes these data further according to the four types of diction, and compares the results we have given previously for C in Table 6:

TABLE 13

INDEXED LANGUAGE IN C' PASSAGES, BY TYPE

passage and type diction	number of instances		number of indices		% of total number of words	
	C'	C	C'	C	C'	C
3:6-13						
I:	4	4	4	4	12%	10%
7:1-8:3						
I:	17	17	13	13	11%	10%
II:	10	10	7	7	7%	6%
III:	6	6	6	6	4%	4%
IV:	16	22	12	15	11%	14%

TABLE 13 (Continued)

passage and type diction	number of instances		number of indices		% of total number of words	
	C'	C	C'	C	C'	C
11:1-14						
I:	7	9	7	7	12%	13%
II:	9	10	5	5	9%	8%
III:	2	3	2	3	6%	6%
IV:	2	4	2	4	6%	7%
16:1-15						
I:	6	6	4	4	10%	9%
II:	2	2	2	2	3%	3%
III:	3	4	3	4	12%	12%
IV:	3	5	3	4	6%	8%
17:19-27						
I:	1	1	1	1	1%	1%
II:	2	2	2	2	7%	7%
IV:	5	5	5	5	6%	6%
18:1-12						
I:	3	3	3	3	7%	6%
II:	1	1	1	1	3%	3%
IV:	3	5	2	4	8%	12%
19:2b-9 11b-13						
I:	2	2	2	2	4%	4%
II:	4	4	4	4	8%	8%
III:	3	3	3	3	9%	8%
IV:	2	4	2	3	5%	8%
21:1-10						
I:	1	1	1	1	3%	2%
III:	1	2	1	2	3%	5%
IV:	4	5	4	4	10%	10%
22:1-5						
I:	1	1	1	1	5%	5%
III:	1	1	1	1	4%	4%
IV:	2	2	2	2	13%	13%
25:1-14						
I:	6	7	6	6	12%	10%
II:	2	2	2	1	4%	3%
III:	1	1	1	1	1%	1%
IV:	4	7	3	6	9%	10%

TABLE 13 (Continued)

passage and type diction	number of instances		number of indices		% of total number of words	
	C'	C	C'	C	C'	C
27:1-22						
II:	0	1	0	1	0%	1%
IV:	6	14	3	9	5%	10%
29:1-32						
I:	2	4	2	4	1%	2%
II:	0	1	0	1	0%	1%
III:	0	4	0	3	0%	2%
IV:	3	12	3	7	2%	6%
32:1-44						
I:	16	17	15	16	7%	6%
II:	6	6	6	6	3%	3%
III:	3	4	3	4	1%	2%
IV:	7	11	7	9	4%	5%
33:1-26						
I:	0	3	0	3	0%	3%
II:	0	1	0	1	0%	1%
III:	2	3	1	1	2%	2%
IV:	4	5	3	3	7%	4%
34:1-22						
I:	3	4	3	3	4%	4%
II:	1	2	1	2	1%	2%
III:	3	3	3	3	3%	2%
IV:	4	8	3	5	6%	7%
35:1-9						
I:	7	7	7	7	8%	6%
II:	1	1	1	1	1%	1%
IV:	6	12	6	8	6%	11%
39:15-18						
IV:	0	1	0	1	0%	6%
44:1-14						
I:	5	6	5	6	5%	4%
II:	6	7	2	3	8%	8%
III:	1	1	1	1	1%	1%
IV:	6	11	5	6	6%	12%
45:1-5						
I:	1	1	1	1	4%	3%
IV:	1	1	1	1	10%	9%

For the majority of passages the types of diction employed are the same in C' as in C, but there are four significant differences. The shortest passage (39:15-18) has no indexed diction at all in C'. Three of the longer passages (all more than 400 words) employ fewer types in C' (27:1-22 lacks Type II, and so employs only Type IV; 29:1-32 lacks Types II and III; 33:1-26 lacks Types I and II). In fact, two of the passages which have Dtr diction in C lack it in C' (27:1-22 and 33:1-26).

Diction which is attested in Dtr (Types I and II) constitutes more than half of the indexed language of nine passages in C', compared to five in C (the additional passages are 7:1-8:3; 18:1-12; 35:1-19; and 44:1-14). This is also the case for diction which is not attested in Dtr or Deuteronomy (Type IV) in six passages in C', compared to eight in C (there is one additional passage, 33:1-26; but three others no longer belong in this category in C': 18:1-12, 29:1-32, and 35:1-19).

The results are similar when we look for unusually high or low percentages. In C', Types I and II constitute 10 percent or more of the language of nine passages, compared to six in C (the additional passages are 16:1-15, 18:1-12, and 32:1-44). This is true of Type IV diction in only four passages, compared to eight in C (there is one additional passage, 45:1-5, but five others no longer belong in this category in C': 18:1-12, 25:1-14, 27:1-22, 35:1-19, and 44:1-14). The number of passages in which Types I and II constitute less than 5 percent of the language is unchanged (six in C' and C), but there are four passages in which this is true of Type IV diction in C', compared to two in C.

In summary, what we have observed about the C' corpus as a whole is true of many individual passages: diction attested in Dtr is more prominent and constitutes a larger percentage of the language than it does in C, while diction which is not attested in Dtr or Deuteronomy is less prominent and constitutes a smaller percentage of the language. We therefore drew the inference that C' stands closer to Dtr than C does. The likeness of C to Dtr is not the result of the expansion it has undergone.

DEUTERONOMISTIC DICTION IN THE READINGS OF C+

Something of the general character of C+ (the text peculiar to the MT) can be inferred from what we have already said in comparing C' (the common text) to C (the MT). The diction of C+ can be seen most clearly, however, when it is compared to C'. The following table uses the ratio of the lengths of C' to C+ which we have established in Table 7:

TABLE 14

INSTANCES OF INDEXED DICTION IN C+ AND C'

	C'	C+
a. total number of instances:	230	82
b. comparative lengths of texts:	3.94	1.00
c. weighted number of instances (a. divided by b.):	58 *	82
d. the percentage by which C+ exceeds C':		41%

In C+ indexed words and phrases are 41 percent more frequent per unit of text: 230 instances in C', but 82 instances in C+, which has only one-fourth as much text. So it appears that C+ spoke in clichés and conventional language significantly more than C'.

The following table shows how these indexed words and phrases are distributed in C' and C+.

TABLE 15

INDEXED WORDS AND PHRASES IN C' AND C+

type of diction:	I	II	III	IV	total
words and phrases employed only by C':	28	9	10	8	55
words and phrases employed only by C+:	2	0	1	3	6
words and phrases employed by both:	7	4	6	14	31
	37	13	17	25	92

It is apparent from Table 15 that the overall tendency of C+ to make more frequent use of indexed language does not hold true for Deuteronomistic diction in particular; of the forty-eight different Dtr words and

phrases (Types I and II) we have identified in C' (i.e., the total number of
Dtr indices [50] minus the two that are peculiar to C+), eleven are to be
found in C+, which is what one would expect given the comparative length
of the materials; two others are added by C+ (i.e., words and phrases
employed by C+). In contrast, C+ employs fourteen of the twenty-two
Type IV words and phrases attested in C'. This is four higher than one
would expect, given the comparative lengths of C+ and C', and supports
that the conventional language of C+ is less directly associated with Dtr
than the conventional language of C'.

A comparison by the number of instances of indexed diction shows
similar results. Table 16 provides the data for C+, and compares these to
the data given for C' in Table 11:

TABLE 16

INSTANCES OF INDEXED DICTION IN C' AND C+, BY TYPE OF DICTION

type of diction:	I	II	III	IV	total
number of instances in C':	82	44	26	78	230
number of instances in C+:	11	6	9	56	82
*number of instances weighted according to a 3.94:1.00 ratio of C':C+					
C':	21^*	11^*	7^*	20^*	59
C+:	11	6	9	56	82
	1.9:1	1.8:1	1:1.3	1:2.8	1:1.4
percentage of total for C':	36%	19%	11%	34%	100%
percentage of total for C+:	13%	7%	11%	68%	100%

Note that Dtr diction is employed 17 times in C+, but 126 times in C';
since C' has four times the material, this means that per unit of text
there are about two instances of Dtr diction in C' for every one in C+ (a
ratio of 1.9:1). The difference emerges even more clearly when we compare the percentage of the total instances of indexed language: Dtr diction is only 21 percent of the indexed language to be found in C+ (17 of 82

instances), but 55 percent of the indexed language to be found in C' (126 of 230 instances). Some of the instances in C+ are demonstrably derivative: C+ has simply taken a word or a phrase which already appears in the C' passage and introduced it another time.[2] All this surely indicates that C+ was not nearly as steeped in Dtr diction as C' had been; the association with Dtr, relatively strong in C', is significantly weaker in C+.

It is immediately evident from Table 16 that what C+ does multiply in the text are those indices which are not expressly Dtr or Deuteronomic (Type IV). The vast majority of these non-Dtr/Deuteronomic words and phrases are already attested in C'; C+ adds only three new phrases of this sort (see Table 15). But this Type IV diction represents fully 68 percent of the total number of instances of indexed language in C+, while it represents only 34 percent (i.e., precisely half) of the total number in C' (56 of 82 in C+ but 78 of 230 in C'; see Table 16). In this case the difference is particularly striking when we compare the number of instances: there are seventy-eight instances of Type IV diction in C', but fifty-six in C+, in one-fourth the text. This means that per unit of text there are about eleven instances in C+ for every four in C' (a ration of 2.8:1). Here again some of this diction is obviously derivative; a word or phrase which already appears in the passage in C' has been introduced once (or twice) more by C+.[3]

It appears from these observations that C+ tends to draw much of its stilted diction from C', which is the text it is expanding and elaborating. If there are other formulae or formulaic expressions peculiar to it, by which it could be recognized, our analysis has not found them, and they are not to be discovered by looking for diction drawn from Dtr. C+ is obviously enamored of the rhetorical style of C', which it imitates and even intensifies. But C+ has no special eye for Dtr diction, and evidently no particular interest in it; otherwise it would surely have chosen this language in particular to replicate.[4] Much of the Dtr diction found in C+ is no doubt derivative from C'; the expanded text shows no independent development of this language, or else it would have employed more idioms which do not appear already in C'.

---

[2] For example, 11:7 from 11:4; 25:7 from 25:6.

[3] For example, 19:9 from 19:7; 21:9 from 21:7; 29:21 from 29:9.

[4] Our finds do not support those of E. Tov, who has argued that C+ has undergone a Deuteronomistic redaction. Our judgment holds true not only for the MT plusses to the prose sermons (= C+) but also for the MT plusses to the remaining strata in the book (see n. 5 below).

There is therefore every reason to conclude that the strikingly Deuteronomistic diction of the prose sermons belongs properly to an earlier
stage, before the expansions of C+ revised C' in the line of tradition
represented by the MT, and prior to the divergence of the text traditions
represented by the MT and OG *Vorlage*.[5]

---

[5]The MT plusses in the other parts of the book of Jeremiah show even
less interest in Deuteronomistic or Deuteronomic diction. Such diction
represents less than 2 percent of the total number of additional words in
the MT (35 of 1996 words, using Min's statistics as database). There are
only twelve Dtr or Deuteronomic phrases which are MT additions. The one
in 44:29, however, has probably been omitted in the OG by homoeoteleuton; the scribe skipped from the first instance of ʿlykm to the second,
leaving out the intervening words. Two occur in the so-called "oracles
against foreign nations" (48:47 *wšbty šbwt*; 49:6 *ʾšyb (ʾt) šbwt*); two others
occur in the historical appendix (52:2 *wyʿś hrʿ bʿyny yhwh*; 52:3 *hšlykw . . .
mʿl pnyw*). Six Dtr or Deuteronomic phrases appear in the "A" and "B"
layers of the book (13:10 *hhlkym bšrrwt lbm*; 23:22 *wyšbwm mdrkm hrʿ*;
25:18 *kywm hzh*; 28:16 *ky srh dbrt ʾl yhwh*; 40:12 *ʾšr ndḥw šm*; 44:23 *kywm
hzh*)̦ one occurs within the context of the oracles of hope (30:22 *whyytm
ly lʿm*).

EXCURSUS

Additional Remarks on the Character of C+

Having ascertained the type of diction most frequently employed by C+ and drawn several conclusions from it, we turn now to other characteristic features of C+ as a supplementary text. The vast majority of the additions of C+, as we have seen have no significant bearing on the subject-matter in C'. They are essentially elaborations of the text. As Tov has remarked, the editor of the MT shows an amazing ability "to insert the new elements . . . between the existing part of ed[ition] I [our C'] without introducing significant changes."[6] These new elements may be summarized as follows:[7]

(1) C+ very often inserts adjectival, adverbial, and appositional modifiers which serve to clarify, stress, or qualify existing parts of C' (e.g., 7:13, 26; 8:3; 16:13; 25:11; 27:6, 8, 16; 32:36, 43).

(2) C+ very often provides supplementary titles and names which are already known in C' (e.g., 21:2, 4; 27:20 [twice]; 29:3, 21, 32; 32:1, 2, 3, 4).

(3) C+ supplies additional epithets for the divine name in prophetic formulae, frequently filling them out to the full form yhwh ṣbʾwt ʾlhy yśrʾl (7:21; 16:9; 19:3; 29:8; passim) and occasionally to shorter forms (21:4; 25:8; 33:4; 34:2). The text also introduces and fills out prophetic formulae, most often nʾm yhwh, but also kh ʾmr yhwh (e.g., 3:10; 7:13, 20 [ʾdny yhwh]; 8:3 [nʾm yhwh ṣbʾwt]; 18:5, 11 [lʾmr kh ʾmr yhwh]; 21:10; 25:7, 12; 27:11, 21 [kh ʾmr yhwh ṣbʾwt ʾlhy yśrʾl]; 29:9, 32).

(4) Implicit pronominal suffixes are occasionally made explicit (18:4 [twice]; 29:32; 32:9, 12; 33:5; 34:3; 35:5, 12; cf. 34:1).

(5) Stock phrases, Type IV clichés, and serial clauses are often extended to a fuller form by C+. These conventional phrases and clauses are often pejorative in nature (e.g., 16:4, 6; 18:7, 11; 19:9; 21:5, 9; 25:11, 12; 27:5, 8; 32:19, 24; 33:12, 35:17; 44:10, 11, 12).

(6) C+ inserts short verbal sentences—simple interpolations—which are both conjunctive and disjunctive in nature. These are usually introduced without modifiers. They serve most often to accentuate the idea which immediately precedes or follows (3:9; 19:5; 21:4, 7; 25:3, 6; 27:10; 29:12; 44:2, 17; 35:2; 44:10).

---

[6]Tov, "Exegetical," p. 88.

[7]For a characterization of additions in Jer-MT as a whole, see Min, "Minuses and Pluses," pp. 255f.; Janzen, *Studies*, pp. 127f.

(7) In several instances the additions of C+ occur at the beginning and the end of a passage (or section of a passage), providing an overall framework for C' (7:1f., 8:3; 21:10; 25:14; 27:1, 22; 29:32; 32:44; 35:19; in 35:19 C+ inserts *lkn kh ʾmr yhwh ṣbʾwt ʾlhy yśrʾl* immediately prior to the concluding words in C').

Certain materials introduced by C+ do supply new subject-matter or modify the sense of the text. These usually take the form of complex phrases, sentences, or extended passages. The ideas which are introduced or modified in this way can be summarized as follows:

(1) C+ occasionally provides new information concerning location, historical setting, or other circumstantial detail (7:1-15 [see p. 58 above]; 25:1b; 27:1, 7, 16 [ʿth mhrh], 20 [cf. 28:4], 22; 32:5b; 34:8, 19, 22 [see pp. 102f. above ; 44:1 [wbnp], 11f.).

(2) In C+ Nebuchadnezzar plays a significantly more prominent role in Judah's experience than is true of C'. He is often mentioned by name or title (21:2, 4, 7; 25:1b, 11, 12, 9; 27:8, 12, 14, 20; 29:3, 21; 32:28; 34:3), is referred to as Yahweh's instrument of punishment (21:4, 7; 25:9, 11; 27:7, 8, 12, 13, 14, 17; 32:28), and is known as Yahweh's servant (25:9; 27:6; see also 43:10); after he executes judgment upon the people of God, he will then in turn be punished by Yahweh (25:11; 27:7).

(3) The explicit rejection of Zedekiah and those with him in Jerusalem (29:16-20) is accentuated by the supplementary text; this long prose saying apparently serves as an implicit salvation pronouncement for the *golah* in Babylon (cf. 24:1-10; see also pp. 00 below).

(4) In C+ it is Jerusalem, rather than the Davidic ruler (23:5f), who bears the title yhwh *ṣdqnw* (33:16), in this way reapplying an oracle originally intended for an individual to the city or perhaps to the community.

(5) In C+ Yahweh promises an unbroken succession of Davidic rulers (33:17).

(6) Yahweh also promises a perpetual succession of Levitical priests (33:18) and, implicitly, a continuing sacrificial cultus (vs. 18) in C+.

By examining the kinds of materials edited in C' as well as those passages around which the editorial remarks cluster, it is possible to say something about the interests, concerns, and *Tendenz* of C+. Admittedly many of the shorter additions of C+ are entirely stylistic in nature and do not reveal anything of its *Anschauung,* but longer plusses and clusters of shorter additions allow us to recognize certain patterns and ideas which appear rather frequently. The additions of C+ often occur in a context of judgment, where the prophet accuses the people of rebellion and disobedience. The long plus in 11:7f. takes the form of a short *unheilsgeschichtliche* credo which characterizes the historical experience of Israel as one of incessant indocility (*wylkw ᵓyš bšryrwt lbm*) and disregard for the word of God. In 29:16-20 C+ introduces the same theme in an even more penetrating manner. Zedekiah and the people residing with him in Jerusalem are accused of rejecting the word of God spoken by his servants, the prophets (vs. 19). Judgment is therefore inevitable. The additions in 3:9; 21:7; 32:30; 35:17; 44:3, 10, 11f. all describe aspects of Judah's apostasy and disobedience to Yahweh and the judgment which such conduct entailed. The sentence added in 7:27 is not simply a reiteration of this motif but a further development of it. C+ seems to suggest here that Judah's apostate and disobedient response to the prophets of old has become so ingrained that their response to Jeremiah's proclamation is entirely predictable (*wlᵓ yšmᶜw ᵓlyk wqrᵓt ᵓlyhm wlᵓ yᶜnwkh*).

For C+, the exile of the people of God from Jerusalem to Babylon is part of the programme of Yahweh for Judah at that particular moment in its history. While the exile is still on the horizon, the additions of C+ focus primarily upon Israel's disobedience and rebellion, and on the impending judgment. As the exile approaches (chapters 25, 27, 29, 32, 34), the emphasis changes to Yahweh's great plan, which includes Babylon and its king to whom the people of God are to be subjugated. In this respect C+ seems to be *golah*-oriented, inasmuch as it accentuates the role of Babylon and its king in the divine programme and favors the exiles in Babylon over against Zedekiah and those with him in Jerusalem. C+ strongly entreats the people of Judah to submit to the rule of Nebuchadnezzar, which is evidently thought to represent Yahweh's will for them at that particular point in their historical experience (27:12-14, 17). In Jer. 29:1-32, Yahweh promises mercy to the *golah in Babylon* while at the same time he announces his utter rejection of Zedekiah and those residing with him *in Jerusalem*. In vv. 1b (*ᵓšr hglh nbwkdn ᵓ ṣr myrwšlm bblh*), 4 (*bblh*), and 6 (*šm,* referring to Babylon) C+ reveals its interest in Babylon, for it is in Babylon that Yahweh's future programme of salvation is to unfold. In C' the exiles in Babylon are promised good fortune if they will become peaceful subjects of the foreign powers; they are assured of restoration and eventual return to Jerusalem (vs. 10 C', vs. 14 C+). To this plan of salvation (*Heilsplan*) for the *golah* in Babylon, C+ adds that Yahweh will apportion judgment, doom, and destruction to the Davidic ruler (Zedekiah) and those remaining with him in Jerusalem (bᶜyr, vs. 16). C+ uses conventional maledictions, cast in the first person, to convey Yahweh's displeasure with those who did not go to Babylon but instead stayed in Jerusalem. For example, Yahweh himself is said to act as the antagonist who is about to destroy the residents of Jerusalem "by sword, famine, and pestilence" (vs. 18). Over against this thoroughly negative pronouncement upon Zedekiah and the inhabitants of Jerusalem, Yahweh reiterates his promise to restore the fortunes and gather the exiles in Babylon from all the nations where they have been scattered (vs. 14). Thus, while those remaining in the land of Judah are to be scattered and annihilated by Yahweh, those exiled to Babylon are to be gathered and restablished by him. According to C+, Zedekiah and the inhabitants of Jerusalem deserve their punishment because they have not obeyed Yahweh's word spoken by his prophets (vs. 19). The word of Yahweh spoken by the prophets (vs. 19) stands in direct contrast with the lying word (*dbr* . . . *šqr* in vv. 23; 27:14, 16, passim) proclaimed by the "false prophets" of Yahweh. By *dbr šqr* (lie, falsehood), the passages seem to refer to the anti-Babylonian oracle which was intended at first to encourage the people's hopes for a successful resistance to Babylon and subsequently for a prompt return from exile. The "true" word of Yahweh rejected by Zedekiah and those with him in Jerusalem by all indications refers to the prophetic appeal to go to Babylon and submit to the "yoke of Nebuchadnezzar." Since it was Yahweh's will to exile the people of God to Babylon, those remaining in Jerusalem had to face his unconditional rejection as a result of their disobedience. This *golah*-orientation is reinforced in 44:11-14 (where a cluster of plusses occurs) by emphasizing Yahweh's displeasure and rejection of "all Judah" (vs. 11) and the remnant of Judah who have set their faces to "sojourn" to the land of Egypt.

5

Conclusion: A Summary of Findings and Inferences

Although we have noted throughout that there is a great deal of variation from passage to passage, it has been possible to draw some general conclusions with respect to the texts of C' and C+. Our findings with respect to C'—the text common to the MT and the OG *Vorlage*, which we regard as generally representative of an earlier literary stage of the corpus prior to the divergence of the two lines of text transmission—may be summarized as follows:

1. The characteristic features of the corpus which have been identified in the longer text of C (MT) and which have been widely regarded as indications of an association with Deuteronomistic literature and tradition are quite fully represented in the shorter text of C'. Relatively few derive from subsequent expansion. However, genre analyses need to be worked through more carefully.

2. In the corpus as a whole there is actually a higher incidence of Deuteronomistic diction, per unit of text, in the shorter text, C', than in the longer text of C.

3. A few passages which some scholars have included in the C corpus employ no Deuteronomistic diction in the text of C' (27:1-22 and 33:1-26; 39:15-18, which a few have attributed to C, has no such diction even in the MT). One passage (29:1-32) which has little such diction in the MT has even less in C'.

4. None of our findings would contradict the present consensus that there was already a marked affinity between this corpus and Deuteronomistic literature and tradition in the exilic period.

Our findings with respect to C+—the text peculiar to the MT, which we regard as generally representative of subsequent additions to the corpus, introduced after the divergence of the two lines of text transmission—may be summarized as follows:

1. The characteristic diction which has been identified in C appears

more frequently, per unit of text, in C+ than it does in C'. In this respect the language of C+ is even more conventional.

2. This diction is largely derivative, however, and is drawn from the text which is being elaborated (C'). There are few words and phrases commonly regarded as characteristic of C which appear only in C+.

3. This diction is generally less Deuteronomistic than the diction of C'. Deuteronomistic words and phrases are a smaller part of its language, and there are few which could be said to have been drawn independently from Deuteronomy or the Deuteronomistic literature.

4. Instead, C+ tends to employ words and phrases which appear already in the text of C' and which may perhaps be said to resemble Deuteronomistic diction, but are not actually attested in Deuteronomistic literature. This means that the use of Dtr diction to identify later additions to the prose sermons now proves to be misguided. Later additions are marked instead by their tendency to multiply those clichés in C' which are not explicitly Deuteronomistic.

5. The observation that Deuteronomistic diction is less prominent in C+ than in the text it was elaborating is surely an indication that these additions derive from a time or a locale in which the Deuteronomistic literature was not the primary focus of attention or study.

6. C+ tends to sympathize more with the exiles in Babylon than with those who remained behind in the land, and the promises it introduces or elaborates are often focused upon their return. It is unlikely that this viewpoint reflects the situation of the sixth century, because it is difficult to suppose that the two text traditions had diverged so early. One might think of a provenience in Babylon later, among the exiles who remained, but the emphasis upon a return to Jerusalem seems to speak against this. It is more likely to reflect the viewpoint of the repatriates who had returned to Judea and who saw themselves as the heirs of the promise.

Selected Bibliography

Ackroyd, Peter R. *Exile and Restoration.* Philadelphia: Westminster Press, 1968.

Arndt, W. F., and Gingrich, F. W. *A Greek-English Lexicon of the New Testament.* London: Cambridge Press, 1957.

Barr, James. *The Semantics of Biblical Language.* London: Oxford, 1961.

Baumann, Eberhart. "šwb šbwt. Eine exegetische Untersuchung." *ZAW* (1929) 17-44.

Berridge, John. *Prophet, People, and the Word of Yahweh: An Examination of Form and Content in the Proclamation of the Prophet Jeremiah.* Zurich: EVZ-Verlag, 1970.

Boecker, Hans Jochen. *Redeformen des Rechtslebens im Alten Testament.* Wissenschaftliche Monographien zum Alten und Neuen Testament 14. 2nd ed. Wageningen: Neukirchener, 1970.

Brekelmans, Chr. "Some Considerations on the Prose Sermons in the Book of Jeremiah." *Bijdragen Tijdschrift voor Filosophie en Theologie* 34 (1973) 204-11.

Bright, John. "The Book of Jeremiah. Its Structure, its Problems, and their Significance for the Interpreter." *Interpretation* 9 (1955) 259-78.

_____ "The Date of the Prose Sermons of Jeremiah," *JBL* 70 (1951) 15-35.

_____ *A History of Israel.* Philadelphia: Westminster Press, 1976.

_____ *Jeremiah. Introduction, Translation, and Notes.* Anchor Bible. New York: Doubleday and Company, 1965.

_____ "The Prophetic Reminiscence: Its Place and Function in the Book of Jeremiah." In *Proceedings of the Ninth Meeting. Die Ou-Testamentiese Werkgemeenskap in Suid-Afrika,* pp. 11-30. Pretoria, 1967.

Brown, F., Driver, S. R., and Briggs, C. A. *A Hebrew and English Lexicon of the Old Testament.* London: Oxford, 1959.

Cazelles, H. "Jeremie et la Deutéronome." *Rechercher de Science Religieuses* 38 (1951) 5-36.

Colenso, J. W. *The Pentateuch and the Book of Joshua Critically Examined.* Part 7. London, 1879.

Cornill, C. H. *Das Buch Jeremia.* Leipzig: C. H. Tauchnitz, 1905.

Cross, Frank M. "The Contribution of the Qumran Discoveries to the Study of the Biblical Text." In *Qumran and the History of the Biblical Text,* pp. 278-92. Edited by Frank M. Cross and Shemaryahu Talmon. Cambridge: Harvard University Press, 1975.

_____ "The History of the Biblical Text in the Light of Discoveries in the Judaean Desert." In *Qumran and the History of the Biblical Text,* pp. 177-95. Edited by F. M. Cross and S. Talmon. Cambridge: Harvard University Press, 1975.

_____ "The Themes of the Book of Kings and the Structure of the Deuteronomistic History," In *Canaanite Myth and Hebrew Epic.* Cambridge: Harvard University Press, 1973.

Dahood, Mitchell. "Philological Notes on Jer 18:14-15." *ZAW* 74 (1962) 207-9.

David, Martin. "The Manumission of Slaves under Zedekiah: A Contribution to the Laws about Hebrew Slaves." *Oudtestamentische Studiën* 5 (1948) 63-79.

Duhm, Bernhard. *Das Buch Jeremia.* Kurzer Hand-Commentar zum Alten Testament, 11. Tübingen and Leipzig: J. C. B. Mohr, 1901.

Eichrodt, Walther. "The Right Interpretation of the Old Testament. A Study of Jeremiah 7:1-15." *Theology Today* 7 (1950) 15-25.

Eissfeldt, Otto. *The Old Testament: An Introduction.* Translated by Peter R. Ackroyd. New York: Harper & Row, 1965.

Elliger, Karl, and Rudolph, Wilhelm. *Biblia Hebraica Stuttgartensia.* 4th ed. Stuttgart: Württembergische Bibelanstalt Stuttgart, 1977.

Erbt, Wilhelm. *Jeremia und seine Zeit. Die Geschichte der letzten fünfzig Jahre des vorexilischen Juda.* Göttingen: Vandenhoeck and Ruprecht, 1902.

Fohrer, Georg. "Jeremias Tempelwort 7:1-15." *Theologische Zeitschrift* 5 (1949) 401-17.

Giesebrecht, F. *Das Buch Jeremia.* Handkommentar zum Alten Testament, III.2. 2nd ed. Göttingen: Vandenhoeck and Ruprecht, 1907.

Graf, Karl Heinrich. *Der Prophet Jeremia.* Leipzig: T. O. Weigel, 1862.

Granild, Sigurd. "Jeremia und das Deuteronomium." *Studia Theologica* 16 (1962) 135-54.

Hatch, Edwin, and Redpath, Henry A. *A Concordance to the Septuagint and the Other Greek Versions of the Old Testament.* 2 vols. Oxford: Clarendon Press, 1897.

Herrmann, Siefried. "Forschung am Jeremiabuch." *Theologische Literaturzeitung* 102 (1977) 481-90.

_____ *Die prophetischen Heilserwartungen im Alten Testament.* Beiträge zur Wissenschaft vom Alten und Neuen Testament 5. Stuttgart: W. Kohlhammer Verlag, 1965.

Hitzig, Ferdinand. *Der Prophet Jeremia.* Kurzgefasstes exegetisches Handbuch zum Alten Testament, III. Leipzig: S. Hirzel, 1866.

Hobbs, Thomas R. "Some Remarks on the Composition and Structure of the Book of Jeremiah." *CBQ* 34 (1974) 257-75.

Holladay, William L. "A Fresh Look at 'Source B' and 'Source C' in Jeremiah." *VT* 25 (1975) 394-412.

_____ "Jeremiah and Moses: Further Observations." *JBL* 85 (1966) 17-27.

_____ *Jeremiah: Spokesman out of Time.* Philadelphia: Pilgrim Press, 1974.

_____ "'On every high hill and under every green tree.'" *VT* 11 (1961) 170-76.

_____ "Prototype and Copies: A New Approach to the Poetry Prose Problem in the Book of Jeremiah." *JBL* 79 (1960) 351-67.

_____ "The so-called 'Deuteronomic gloss' in Jer 8:19b." *VT* 12 (1962) 494-98

_____ "Style, Irony, and Authenticity in Jeremiah." *JBL* 81 (1962) 44-54.

Hölscher, Gustav. *Die Profeten: Untersuchungen zur Religionsgeschichte Israels.* Leipzig: R. Voightlanders Verlag, 1914.

Horst, Friedrich. "Die Anfänge des Propheten Jeremia." *ZAW* 41 (1923) 94-153.

Horwitz, William J. "Audience Reaction to Jeremiah." *CBQ* 32 (1970) 555-64.

Huffmon, Herbert B. "The Covenant Lawsuit in the Prophets." *JBL* 78 (1959) 285-95.

Hyatt, J. Philip. "The Beginning of Jeremiah's Prophecy." *ZAW* 78 (1966) 204-14.

_____ *The Book of Jeremiah.* Interpreter's Bible 5, pp. 775-1142. New York: Abingdon, 1956.

_____ "The Deuteronomic Edition of Jeremiah." *Vanderbilt Studies in the Humanities* 1 (1951) 71-95.

_____ "Jeremiah and Deuteronomy." *Journal of Near Eastern Studies* 1 (1942) 156-73.

_____ "The Original Text of Jeremiah 11:15-16." *JBL* 60 (1941) 57-60.

Jacoby, Georg, "Zur Komposition des Buches Jeremia." *Theologische Studien und Kritiken* 79 (1906) 1-30.

Janssen, Enno. *Juda in der Exilszeit. Ein Beitrag zur Frage der Entstehung des Judentums.* Forschungen zur Religion und Literatur des Alten und Neuen Testaments 69. Göttingen: Vandenhoeck and Ruprecht, 1956.

Janzen, John G. "Double Readings in the Text of Jeremiah." *Harvard Theological Review* 60 (1967) 433-47.

_____ *Studies in the Text of Jeremiah.* Harvard Semitic Monograph 6. Cambridge: Harvard University Press, 1973.

Jellicoe, Sidney. *The Septuagint and Modern Study.* Oxford: Clarendon Press, 1968.

Jepsen, Alfred. *Die Quellen des Konigsbuches.* Halle, 1953.

Johnstone, W. "The Setting of Jeremiah's Prophetic Activity." *Transactions of the Glasgow University Oriental Society* 21 (1965)/6) 47-55.

Kaiser, Otto. *Introduction to the Old Testament.* Translated by John Sturdy. Minnesota: Augsburg Publishers, 1977.

Kessler, Martin. "Jeremiah Chapters 26-45 Reconstructed." *Journal of Near Eastern Studies* 27 (1968) 81-88.

_____ "The Laws of Manumission in Jer 34." *Bibl. Zeitschrift,* NF, 15 (1971) 105-8.

_____ "A Prophetic Biography: A Form-Critical Study of Jeremiah. Chapters 26-29, 32-45." Ph.D. dissertation, Brandeis University, 1965.

Klein, Ralph W. *Textual Criticism of the Old Testament: The Septuagint after Qumran.* Philadelphia: Fortress Press, 1974.

Köhler, Ludwig, and Baumgartner, Walter. *Lexicon in Veteris Testamenti Libros.* Leiden: E. J. Brill, 1958.

Kuenen, Abraham. *Historisch-kritische Einleitung in die Bücher des Alten Testament II: Die prophetischen Bucher.* Leipzig, 1892.

Lemche, N. P. "The Manumission of Slaves—the Fallow Year—the Sabbatical Year—the Jobel Year." *VT* 26 (1976) 38-59.

Lemke, W. E. "Nebuchadrezzar, My Servant." *CBQ* 28 (1966) 45-50.

Leslie, Elmer A. *Jeremiah. Chronologically arranged, translated, and interpreted.* New York and Nashville: Abingdon Press, 1954.

Liddell, H. G. and Scott, R. *A Greek-English Lexicon.* Revised by H. S. Jones. Oxford: Clarendon Press, 1940.

Lindblom, Johannes. *Prophecy in Ancient Israel.* Philadelphia: Fortress Press, 1962.

Lipinski, Edward. "Prose ou poésie en Jér 34:1-7?" *VT* 24 (1974) 112-13.

Lörcher, H. "Das Verhältnis der Prosareden zu dem Erzählungen im Jeremiabuch." Th.D. dissertation, Tübingen, 1974.

Lundbom, J. R. *Jeremiah: A Study of Ancient Hebrew Rhetoric.* Missoula, Montana: Scholars Press, 1975.

May, Herbert Gordon. "Jeremiah's Biographer." *Journal of Bible and Religion* 10 (1942) 195-201.

_____ "Towards an Objective Approach to the Book of Jeremiah: The Biographer." *JBL* 61 (1942) 139-55.

Meinhold, Johannes. *Einführung in das Alten Testament*. 2d ed. Giessen, 1926.

Meyer, Rudolf. *Hebräische Grammatik*. Edition 3: *Satzlehre*. 3. neubearb. Aufl. Sammlung Göschen. Berlin: Walter Gruyter, 1972.

Milgrom, Jacob. "Concerning Jeremiah's Repudiation of Sacrifice: A Reply to Weinfeld." *ZAW* 89 (1977) 273-75.

Miller, John Wolf. *Das Verhältnis Jeremias und Hesekiels sprachlich und theologisch Untersucht*. Assen: Royal VanGorcum Ltd., 1955.

Minetta DeTillesse, G. "Sections 'tu' et sections 'vous' dans le Deutéronome." *VT* 12 (1962) 29-87.

Mowinckel, Sigmund. *Prophecy and Tradition: The Prophetic Books in the light of Study of the Growth and History of the Tradition*. Oslo: Jacob Dybwad, 1946.

_____ *Zur Komposition des Buches Jeremia*. Kristiania: Jacob Dybwad, 1914.

Muilenburg, James. "The Form and Structure of the Covenant Formulations." *VT* 9 (1959) 347-65.

_____ "Jeremiah." *Interpreter's Dictionary of the Bible*. Vol. 2. New York and Nashville: Abingdon Press, 1962.

Neumann, P. K. D. "Das Wort, das geschehen . . . . Zum Problem der Wortempfangsterminologie in Jer 1-25." *VT* 23 (1973) 171-217.

Nicholson, Ernest W. *Preaching to the Exiles: A Study of the Prose Tradition in the Book of Jeremiah*. New York: Schocken Books, 1971.

Nötscher, Friedrich, *Das Buch Jeremias*. Die Heilige Schrift des Alten Testaments, VII. 2. Bonn: Hanstein, 1934.

Noth, Martin. *The History of Israel*. Translated by P. R. Ackroyd. 2d edition. New York and Evanston: Harper & Row, 1960.

_____ *Überlieferungsgeschichtliche Studien: Die sammelnden und bearbeitenden Geschichtswerke im Alten Testament*. 3 unveränderte Aufl. Tübingen: Max Niemeyer Verlag, 1967.

_____ "Zur Geschichtsauffassung des Deuteronomisten." *Proceedings of the Twenty-Second Congress of Orientalists*. Volume 2: *Communications*, pp. 558-65. Edited by Zeki Veledi Togan. Leiden: E. J. Brill.

Olmstead, Albert Ten. "Source Study and the Biblical Text." *American Journal of Semitic Languages and Literature* 30 (1913) 1-35.

Osswald, Eva. *Falsche Prophetie im Alten Testament*. Tübingen: J. C. B. Mohr, 1962.

Overholt, Thomas W. "King Nebuchadrezzar in the Jeremiah Tradition." *CBQ* 30 (1968) 39-48.

_____ "Remarks on the Continuity of the Jeremiah Tradition." *JBL* 91 (1972) 457-62.

_____ *The Threat of Falsehood. A Study in the Theology of the Book of Jeremiah*. London: SCM, 1970.

Petersen, D. L. *Late Israelite Prophecy: Studies in Deutero-Prophetic Literature and in Chronicles*. Missoula, Montana: Scholars Press for SBL, 1977.

Pfeiffer, Robert Henry. *Introduction to the Old Testament*. Rev. ed. New York: Harper & Row, 1949.

Podechard, E. "Le livre de Jérémia: structure et formation." *RB* 37 (1928) 181-97.

Pohlmann, Karl-Friedrich. *Studien zum Jeremiabuch. Ein Beitrag zur Frage nach der Entstehung des Jeremiabuches*. Göttingen: Vandenhoeck and Ruprecht, 1978.

von Rad. Gerhard. *Old Testament Theology*. Translated by D. M. G. Stalker. 2 vols. New York, Evanston, San Francisco and London: Harper & Row, 1965.

_____ *Studies in Deuteronomy*. Translated by D. M. G. Stalker. Studies in Biblical Theology, no. 9. London: SCM Press, 1953.

Reventlow, H. Graf. "Gattung und Überlieferung in der 'Templerede Jeremias.'" *ZAW* 81 (1969) 315-52.

Reymond, Philippe. "Sacrifice et 'spiritualité', ou sacrifice et alliance? Jer. 7:22-24." *ThZ* 21 (1965) 314-17.

Riemann, Paul A. "Covenant, Mosaic." *The Interpreter's Dictionary of the Bible, Supplementary Volume*, pp. 192-97. Edited by Keith Crim, gen. ed. Nashville: Abingdon, 1976.

Rietzschel, D. *Das Problem der Urrolle. Ein Beitrag zur Redaktionsgeschichte des Jeremiabuches*. Gütersloh: Gütersloher Verlagshaus, 1966.

Robert, Andres. "Jérémie et la Réforme deutéronomique d'apres Jér. 11:1-14." *Revue des sciences religieuses* 31 (1943) 5-16.

Robinson, Theodore Henry. "Baruch's Roll." *ZAW* 42 (1924) 209-21.

Rose, M. *Der Ausschliesslichkeitsanspruch Jahwes. Deuteronomische Schultheologie und die Volksfrömmigkeit in der späten Konigszeit.* Beiträge zur Wissenschaft vom Alten und Neuen Testament 106. Stuttgart: W. Kohlhammer Verlag, 1975.

Rowley, Harold Henry. "The Prophet Jeremiah and the Book of Deuteronomy." In *Studies in Old Testament Prophecy Presented to Theodore H. Robinson,* pp. 157-74. Edinburgh: T & T Clark, 1950.

Rudolph, Wilhelm. *Jeremia.* Handbuch zum Alten Testament 12. Tübingen: J. C. B. Mohr, 1947.

_____ "Zum Jeremiabuch." *ZAW* 60 (1944) 85-106.

Scholz, Anton. *Der Masorethische Text die LXX-Uebersetzung des Buches Jeremias.* Regensburg: G. J. Manz, 1875.

Seebass, Horst. "Jeremias Konflikt mit Chananja. Bemerkungen zu Jer 27 und 28." *ZAW* 82 (1970) 449-52.

Seitz, G. *Redaktiongeschichtlicht Studien zum Deuteronomium.* Beiträge zur Wissenschaft vom Alten und Neuen Testament 93. Stuttgart: W. Kohlhammer Verlag, 1971.

Sekine, Masao. "Davidsbund und Sinaibund bei Jeremia." *VT* 9 (1959) 47-57.

Skinner, John. *Prophecy and Religion. Studies in the Life of Jeremiah.* Cambridge: University Press, 1922.

Smith, Eustace J. "The Decalogue in the Preaching of Jeremiah." *CBQ* 4 (1942) 197-209.

Snaith, Norman Henry. *Notes on the Hebrew Text of Jeremiah.* London: Epworth Press, 1945.

Stade, Bernhard. "Bemerkungen zum Buche Jeremia." *ZAW* 12 (1892) 276-308.

_____ "Jer. 3:6-16." *ZAW* 4 (1884) 151-54.

_____ "Jer. 32:11-14." *ZAW* 5 (1885) 175-78.

Stone, Pearle Felicia. "The Temple Sermons of Jeremiah." *American Journal of Semitic Languages and Literature* 50 (1933)/4) 73-92.

Streane, A. W. *The Double Text of Jeremiah.* Cambridge: D. Bell and Co., 1896.

Stroud, James. "Obey My Voice: A Form-Critical Study of Selected Prose Speeches from the Book of Jeremiah." Ph.D. thesis, Duke University, 1971.

Sutcliffe, Edmund Felix. "A Gloss in Jeremiah 7:4." *VT* 5 (1955) 313-14.

Talmon, Shemaryahu. "Double Readings in the Masoretic Text." *Textus* 1 (1960) 144-84.

_____ "The Textual Study of the Bible—A New Outlook." In *Qumran and the History of the Biblical Text.* Edited by Frank M. Cross and S. Talmon. Cambridge: Harvard University Press, 1975.

Thiel, Winfried. *Die deuteronomistische Redaktion von Jeremia 1-25.* Wissenschaftliche Monographie zum Alten und Neuen Testament, 41. Wageningen: Neukirchener, 1973.

_____ *Die deuteronomistische Redaktion von Jeremia 26-45.* Düsseldorf: Neukirchener, 1981.

_____ Review of *Preaching to the Exiles,* by Ernest W. Nicholson. *ThLZ* 97 (1972) 25-27.

Tov, Emanuel. "Exegetical Notes on the Hebrew *Vorlage* of the LXX of Jeremiah 27 (34)." *ZAW* 91 (1979) 73-93.

_____ "L'Incidence de la critique textuelle sur la critique littéraire dans la livre de Jérémie." *RB* 79 (1972) 188-99.

_____ "The Nature of the Hebrew Text Underlying the LXX. A Survey of the Problems." *Journal for the Study of the Old Testament* 7 (1978) 53-68.

_____ "On 'Pseudo-Variants' Reflected in the Septuagint." *Journal of Semitic Studies* 20 (1975) 165-77.

_____ "Septuagint." *The Interpreter's Dictionary of the Bible, Supplementary Volume,* pp. 807-11. Edited by Keith Crim, gen. ed. Nashville: Abingdon, 1976.

_____ *The Septuagint Translation of Jeremiah and Baruch. A Discussion of an Early Revision of the LXX of Jeremiah 29-52 and Baruch 1:1-3:8.* Missoula, Montana: Scholars Press, 1976.

_____ "Some Aspects of the Textual and Literary History of the Book of Jeremiah." *Ephemerides Theologicae Lovanienses* 59 (1981) 145-67.

_____ *The Text-Critical Use of the Septuagint in Biblical Research.* Jerusalem: Simor Press, 1982.

Volz, Paul. *Der Prophet Jeremia*. Kommentar zum Alten Testament. Leipzig and Erlangen: A. Deichertsche, 1922.

_____ *Studien zum Text des Jeremia*. Beitrage zur Wissenschaft vom Alten Testament, 25. Leipzig: A. Deichertsche, 1920.

Wambacq, Bernard N. *Jeremias, Klaagliederen, Baruch, Brief van Jeremias*. De Boekan van het Oude Testament, X. Roermond en Maaseik: J. J. Romen & Zonen, 1957.

Weinfeld, Moshe. *Deuteronomy and the Deuteronomic School*. Oxford: Clarendon Press, 1972.

Weippert, Helga. "Jahwekrieg und Bundesfluch in Jer 21:1-7." *ZAW* 82 (1970) 396-409.

_____ *Die Prosareden des Jeremiabuches*. Beiheft zur Zeitschrift für die alttestamentliche Wissenschaft. Berlin: Walter de Gruyter, 1973.

_____ Review of *Preaching to the Exiles,* by Ernest W. Nicholson. *Göttingische Gelehrte Anzeigen* 225 (1973) 1-14.

Weiser, Artur. *Das Buch des Propheten Jeremia*. Das Alte Testament Deutsche, 20-21. 4th ed. Göttingen: Vandenhoeck and Ruprecht, 1960.

Welch, Adam Cleghorn. "Jeremiah's Letter to the Exiles in Babylon." *Expositor* 8 (1921) 358-72.

Wellhausen, J. *Die Composition des Hexateuchs und der historischen Bücher des Alten Testaments*. 4th Ed. Berlin: Walter de Gruyter, 1963.

Weltmen, P. "Leiden und Leidenserfahrung im Buch Jeremia." *ZThK* 74 (1977) 123-50.

Wilcoxen, J. A. "The Political Background of Jeremiah's Temple Sermon." *Scripture in History and Theology* (1977) 151-66.

Wildberger, Hans. *Jahwewort und prophetischen Rede bei Jeremia*. Zürich, 1942.

Wilson, Robert R. *Prophecy and Society in Ancient Israel*. Philadelphia: Fortress Press, 1980.

Workman, G. C. *The Text of Jeremiah*. Edinburgh: T & T Clark, 1889.

Würthwein, Ernst. *The Text of the Old Testament*. Translated by E. F. Rodes, Grand Rapids, Mich.: William B. Eerdmans, 1979.

Ziegler, Joseph. *Beiträge zur Ieremias-Septuaginta*. Göttingen: Vandenhoeck and Ruprecht, 1958.

_____ *Septuaginta, Ieremias, Baruch, Threni, Epistula Ieremiae*.
Vestus Testamentum Graecum, Auctoritate Societatis Litterarum
Gottingensis Editum, vol. 15. Göttingen: Vandenhoeck and Ruprecht,
1957.